ST. CYPRIAN

THE LAPSED
DE LAPSIS

THE UNITY OF THE CATHOLIC CHURCH
DE ECCLESIAE CATHOLICAE UNITATE

ANCIENT CHRISTIAN WRITERS

THE WORKS OF THE FATHERS IN TRANSLATION

EDITED BY

JOHANNES QUASTEN, S. T. D.
Catholic University of America
Washington, D.C.

JOSEPH C. PLUMPE, Ph.D.
Pontifical College Josephinum
Worthington, O.

No. 25

ST. CYPRIAN

THE LAPSED

THE UNITY OF THE CATHOLIC CHURCH

TRANSLATED AND ANNOTATED
BY

MAURICE BÉVENOT, S.J.

D.D. (ROME), M.A. (OXON.)

Mag. Aggr. Pont. Univ. Greg.

Professor of Ecclesiology
Heythrop College, Oxon.

NEWMAN PRESS

New York, N.Y./Ramsey, N.J.

De Licentia Superioris S.J.
  Nihil Obstat
        J. Quasten
            Cens. Dep.

Imprimatur:
        Patricius A. O'Boyle, D.D.
            Archiep. Washingtonen.
                die 2 Nov 1956

Library of Congress
Catalog Card Number: 57-7364

ISBN: 0-8091-0260-9

PUBLISHED BY PAULIST PRESS
Editorial Office: 1865 Broadway, New York, N.Y. 10023
Business Office: 545 Island Road, Ramsey, N.J. 07446

PRINTED AND BOUND IN THE UNITED STATES OF AMERICA

CONTENTS

ST. CYPRIAN

THE LAPSED

THE UNITY OF THE CATHOLIC CHURCH

INTRODUCTION

Caecilius Cyprianus was Bishop of Carthage 249–258. In this short period, he led his flock through a two years' persecution, defended the unity of the Church against two schismatical movements, was the soul of the city's morale during a devastating plague,[1] had a sharp conflict with the Bishop of Rome over the validity of heretical baptism, and was beheaded, a martyr for the faith, in a second persecution.

The two treatises here translated belong to the earlier period of his episcopate, being addresses made to his flock in 251. They deal with the after-effects of the first persecution (that of Decius), which had just finished. During it he had been in hiding, not from any cowardice, but in order that his people might have the direction, the support, and the encouragement which his letters to them and to his clergy could alone provide.[2] On his return among them, his first public address was the De lapsis ('The Lapsed'),[3] in which, while celebrating the return of peace to the Church and rejoicing in the heroism of those martyrs and confessors who had been faithful to Christ, he laid down the obligation of long penance[4] for those who, succumbing to fear or torture, had publicly renounced their faith.

There had been no active persecution since the reign of Septimius Severus (193–211). The Christians had increased in numbers but their fervour had waned, and not a few scandals, even among the higher clergy, showed what might be expected in a fresh outburst of persecution. This came at last with the accession of Decius in 249 who, recognizing the weaknesses within the empire and the dangers which threatened it from the barbarians of the North-East, resolved to re-create its unity by a religious revival, imposing on all his subjects the obligation to offer sacrifice to the gods, to whom were due the glories of the empire in the past. It was this edict under which the Christians suffered. It was not directed primarily against them; it did not aim at their extermination; it did not want to make martyrs (though not a few did die because of it)—it only wanted apostates.[5]

Those who obeyed the edict would present to the officials, appointed for the purpose, a written statement of their having duly taken part in the sacrifice, and they received it back countersigned by them. This was the *libellus*, which gave their name to a definite class of lapsed among the Christians—the *libellatici*. Those who had actually joined in the sacrificial rites were known as *sacrificati*, their having received *libelli* needing no emphasis. The *libellatici*, on the other hand, had not actually sacrificed, but were so called because they had secured, by bribery or otherwise, a *libellus* with the required signature. They tried to salve their conscience by the fact that, after all, it was sacrificing to the gods which was forbidden.

Cyprian made clear to them that such a course, whereby they publicly—if mendaciously—recorded their submission to the edict, was quite as much a denial of their faith as actual participation in the sacrifice would have been. Soon after, both at Carthage and in Rome, the bishops decided that the *libellatici*, who had so far been doing penance, should now be reconciled, and in the following year, when a fresh persecution (under Gallus) was expected, the *sacrificati* too were admitted to Communion, so that they might re-enter the fray refreshed and rearmed. But in the *De lapsis* Cyprian is intent on making clear the guilt not only of the latter, but of the *libellatici* too, who were all too prone to make excuses for themselves. The treatise is a model of pastoral denunciation, combined with exhortation and encouragement to those who keenly felt the disgrace of their fall, or who shrank from the rigours of the Church's penance.[6]

The other treatise, *De ecclesiae catholicae unitate* ('The Unity of the Catholic Church'),[6a] was written within a few months of the first. It is the earliest work on the subject which has survived, and it is not surprising that its treatment of the nature of the Church should seem to us incomplete. Cyprian's whole-hearted conversion, his distribution of his wealth to the poor, and his edifying mode of life had led to his elevation to the episcopate perhaps oversoon. His strong and kindly practical character and his deep religious spirit made him admirably suited for the post; but he had not that long experience of life in the Church which alone would have enabled him to write of the Church not merely in a way adequate to its present needs, but also with that accuracy of touch which would stand the test of time. In his treatise he was meeting the situation as he saw it: we must not expect in it a complete theological treatise on the Church.

What the precise situation was, has been a matter of dispute. Two schisms were at work in 251: that led by the African deacon Felicissimus, and that headed by Novatian, the Roman priest who made himself 'Antipope' in opposition to the newly elected Cornelius. In recent times it has been held that the treatise was written before Novatian's revolt;[7] the older, traditional view is that it was prompted by it and so included both schisms in its scope. The reasons favouring the first view do not seem convincing,[8] and it is here supposed that Novatian had already made attempts to secure recognition in Carthage[9] when Cyprian wrote his treatise and delivered it there. He sent a copy to Rome, where it no doubt played a part in the return of those confessors who had supported Novatian's party.[10]

In the treatise no names are mentioned: the references to the situation are quite general. But chapter 4 presents a *crux*, there being two rival versions of it which have been mixed together in various ways in many MSS. The view here taken is that Cyprian himself revised his text, and that what is known as the 'Primacy Text' (because it contains the word *primatus*) is the original one, whereas the generally received text is his correction of it. This chapter has been the subject of endless controversy, Catholics generally defending the 'primacy' passages against the charge of interpolation, and seeing in them an explicit recognition of the Papal Primacy. But in more recent times, controversy has mostly been replaced by discussion, and the protagonists are no longer divided on strictly denominational lines.[11]

The truth seems to be that though aimed chiefly at Novatian, the intruded Bishop of Rome, the treatise was not meant as a defence of the Papacy as we understand it, but as a defence of the rightful bishop there. In speaking of the 'primacy of Peter' or of 'the Chair of Peter,' Cyprian was not thinking specifically of *Rome*, but literally of Peter and of the *unity* which Christ intended for His Church when He founded it on Peter, and which Novatian was destroying. That unity, in his theory, was constituted simply by the union of the bishops among themselves.

Actually, Cyprian recognized the Bishop of Rome's special position in the Church in many practical ways.[12] But he never formulated this to himself as implying a real authority over the whole Church. Hence, though his practice repeatedly went further than his theory, it is not surprising that, at a moment of crisis, he should have refused to accept the ruling on heretical baptism notified to him by Stephen of Rome. His unwonted vehemence on receiving it shows that he was nonplussed. He had always taken for granted that Carthage and Rome would see eye to eye on any matter of importance: he now found himself in disagreement with Rome on a matter which involved the unity of the Church itself. His theory had, in fact, broken down, but he saw no way out of the impasse. For his instinctive regard for Rome prevented his even considering the only logical course open to him: to break off relations with Rome by excommunicating Stephen.

If he altered the text of chapter 4 (as he seems to have done precisely at this juncture), this will have been *not* because he had changed his mind about the Papacy, but because Rome was reading more into it than he had intended. At Rome, where there were no doubts about its Bishop's authority over the whole Church, Cyprian's original text could not fail to be read as a recognition of that fact. If in the course of the baptismal controversy this was, as it were, thrown in his teeth, he will have exclaimed, quite truthfully: 'But I never meant *that!*'—and so he 'toned it down' in his revised version. He did not, then, repudiate what he had formerly held. He had never held that the Pope possessed universal jurisdiction. But he had never denied it either; in truth he had never asked himself the question where the final authority in the Church might be. The 'union of the bishops' sufficed for all practical purposes—so he thought, at least until the baptismal controversy. It may be that, in the last months of his life, before his martyrdom, he came to realize that his theory of Church unity was only good as far as it went, but that it did not go far enough.[13]

If the foregoing reconstruction is correct, we have in Cyprian's *De ecclesiae catholicae unitate* a good example of what a dogma can look like while still in an early stage of its development. The reality (in this case, the Primacy of Rome) is there all the time : it may be recognized by some; by others it may even be denied, and that though much of what they say or do unconsciously implies it. Such a possibility is not always allowed for; as L. Hertling has well said : 'Those who bandy about the word "development" most are often just those who are least capable of entering into the mind of the men who only knew the dogma in question at an undeveloped stage.'[14] Cyprian is a standing example of what we mean when we speak of the Papal Primacy being 'implicit' in the early Church. That his difference with Rome created no doubts there as to his loyalty to the *unity* of the Church, is shown by his being included in the first Roman 'Martyrology' (A.D. 354), and enshrined for ever in the Canon of the Roman Mass.

✂   ✂   ✂

The controversies that have raged about the name of Cyprian, and especially about his treatise on *The Unity of the Catholic Church*, have obscured the value of his evidence for the Christian life and thought of his period. The majesty of God, His mercy and loving kindness; the mediatorship of Christ, His Son incarnate, and the revelation made manifest in His teaching, His life, death, and resurrection; our dependence on Him for our salvation through Faith, Baptism, the Eucharist, and Penance; His creation of the Church and, within it, of the authority first of the Apostles, then of the bishops their successors, and the necessity of membership of the Church in which He lives on in all its members, and which alone dispenses the gifts of the Spirit; the need of unity and charity in all its forms; the maintenance of a high standard of faith and morality even in the face of the fiercest persecution, and yet a sympathetic understanding for those who have fallen; the future life, prepared for here, determined by Christ's just judgment as eternal happiness or eternal woe —all these features form the background of Cyprian's thought and manifest themselves continually in all his treatises and letters. Equally natural to him is his constant appeal to Scripture: Old and New Testament alike[15] provide him with illustrations or justifications of his teaching and exhortations. And as he is a true pastor of his people, so does he guide his clergy in the difficult times that confront them, and himself promotes, as best he knows, the unity and concord among the bishops of his own African provinces as well as between them and the bishops overseas. His love for Christ and for the Church, as expressed in his writings, enables us to see something of the living Church in action in the middle of the third century.

But in any just estimate of his thought due regard must be had for his style, and this presents certain difficulties to the translator. Cyprian uses all the artifices of the rhetorical schools, and his style has been compared with that of Apuleius, however diverse may have been their subject-matter. 'It would be impossible to show any direct influence of Apuleius on Cyprian, though nothing can be clearer than the fact that both had been trained in the same school of rhetoric. The writers on the style of Apuleius might, with a very small amount of change, turn their books into a treatise on Cyprian. There is only one of Apuleius' devices, the use of diminutives, which is not also employed by Cyprian. . . . The symmetrical arrangement of balanced clauses, the constant pleonasm (for Cyprian when striving to be eloquent will always use two words in preference to one), the alliteration, the rhyme, the poetical diction, the forced metaphors and combinations of incongruous words, and all the artifices of style are to be found in both.'[16] To get his point across, Cyprian will pile words one on top of another, regardless of the nuances between his synonyms, or else he shapes a lapidary dictum—which may sound good, but will not always stand up to close analysis. The general effect is powerful, and his thought reveals itself as strong and often beautiful. But given this *genre* of writing, it is particularly dangerous to isolate particular sentences or phrases from their context, or to build up a system from such phrases gathered from disparate contexts, and call it Cyprian's 'thought.' His Christianity was indeed his life, and he judged all things in its light: this he could do without having any all-embracing preconceived system, and it did not preserve him from occasional inconsistencies.

In his search for accuracy, the translator is tempted to over-emphasize words and phrases which occur incidentally in a general passage; on the other hand, his instinct is to tone down any appearance of inconsistency. If, besides these temptations, the many difficulties inherent in the language itself are borne in mind, as well as the difference in background at a distance of seventeen centuries, it should surprise no one if at times the translation seems involved, or stumbling, or obscure.

ɤ   ɤ   ɤ

The text translated is substantially that of G. Hartel in CORPUS SCRIPTORUM ECCLESIASTICORUM LATINORUM 3.1 (Vienna 1868) 207–64. Its few departures from it depend for the *De lapsis* on J. Martin's edition in the series FLORILEGIUM PATRISTICUM 23 (Bonn 1930), and for the *De ecclesiae catholicae unitate* either on Hartel's own critical apparatus, or (especially in chapter 4) on personal study of the MSS.

The following previous translations have been noted: Thornton, C., *The Treatises of S. Caecilius Cyprian*, in LIBRARY OF THE FATHERS OF THE HOLY CATHOLIC CHURCH 3 (Oxford 1839) 131–76.

Wallis, R. E., *The Writings of Cyprian*, in ANTE-NICENE CHRISTIAN LIBRARY 8 (Edinburgh 1868) 350–98. See the reprint in ANTE-NICENE FATHERS 5 (New York 1907) 421–47.

The *De ecclesiae catholicae unitate* has been separately translated into English—see E. H. Blakeney, with the Latin text (London 1928); O. R. Vassall-Phillips (London 1924); F. A. Wright, *Fathers of the Church: a Selection from the Writings of the Latin Fathers* (London 1928) 112–32 (cf. also 133–37: *De lapsis* §§23–29); into French, with the Latin text, P. de Labriolle (Paris 1942). For further translations into foreign languages, see J. Quasten, *Patrology* 2 (Utrecht–Antwerp 1953) 349 and 352.

However, rightly or wrongly, hardly any use has been made of previous translations in the course of preparing this one. There is therefore no question of the rendering of any passage having been 'preferred' to theirs. At most, some corrections or improvements have been inspired by them in the final revision.

NOTE. *The cross-headings are not in the original.*

THE LAPSED

Joy at the return of peace for the Church and at the triumph of the steadfast (1–3).

1. At last, dear brethren, peace has been restored to the Church and, though the pessimists thought it improbable and the pagans impossible, we have recovered our liberty[1] through the avenging intervention of God.[2] Joy fills our hearts once more and, with the storm-clouds of persecution swept away, the sunshine of calm and tranquillity has returned. We must give praise to God; we must acknowledge His blessings and gifts by our thanksgivings— though in fact our lips never ceased giving thanks even in the midst of persecution; for, however great be the power conceded to the Enemy[3] against us, he can never prevent those who love God with their whole heart and soul and strength from proclaiming His blessings and hymning His praises at all times and places. The day longed for and prayed for by all has come at last, and after a long night of horror and black gloom, the world is bathed in the radiance and splendour of its Lord.

2. Our confessors[4] are a joy to look upon, men whose renown is on every tongue, whose courage and faith have covered them with glory; long have we yearned after them with passionate longing,[5] and we embrace them at last, and affectionately impress on them the sacred kiss.[6] They form the bright army of the soldiers of Christ, whose steadfastness broke the fierce onslaught of persecution, ready as they were for the long-suffering of prison life, steeled to the endurance of death. Valiantly you

13

repudiated the world; to God you offered a glorious spectacle, to your brethren an example to follow. Your pious lips pronounced the name of Christ and acknowledged your unchanging faith in Him;[7] your hands, which none but sacred works had occupied, were kept unsullied by any sacrilegious sacrifice; your lips, sanctified by the food of heaven, would not admit, after Our Lord's body and blood, the contamination of idolatrous sacrifices; your heads retained their freedom from the shameful heathen veil[8] which enslaved the heads of the sacrificers in its folds; your brows, hallowed by God's seal, could not support the wreath of Satan,[9] but reserved themselves for the crown which the Lord would give. With what joy in her breast does Mother Church[10] receive you back from the fray! How blessed, how happy she is to open her gates for you to enter as, in closed ranks, you bear the trophies of the vanquished foe! Joining the victory of their men, come the women too, triumphing over the world and over their sex alike. With them also, celebrating a double victory,[11] come the virgins and boys with virtues beyond their years.

Nay, but the great body of the faithful follow close upon you, having earned titles to glory almost equal to your own. Theirs was the same loyalty of heart, the same integrity of steadfast faith. Rooted unshakably in the laws of God and disciplined in the teachings of the Gospel, they were unmoved by fear at the decrees of banishment, at the tortures awaiting them, or the threats against their property and persons. The date for the testing of their faith had been fixed; but when a man remembers that he has renounced the world, he recognizes no day of the world's fixing; if he looks to an eternity from God, he reckons not the time of earth. 3. Let no one, dear brethren,[12] let no one make little of their glory, let no one with malignant tongue cast a slur on the untarnished courage of those who have stood firm. [13] Once the period prescribed for apostatizing had passed, whoever had failed to declare himself within the time, [14] thereby confessed that he was a Christian. If the primary claim to victory is that, having fallen into the hands of the pagans, a man should confess Our Lord, the next title to glory is that he should have gone underground and preserved himself for God's service. [15] The first makes a public confession, the second a private one; the first wins a victory over an earthly judge, the second keeps his conscience unsullied by the integrity of his will, content to have God as his Judge; in the first, courage is more active, in the second, conscientiousness has inspired prudence. The former, when his hour came, was found to be ripe for it; the hour of the other may only have been postponed since, when he left his estate and went into hiding, he had no intention of denying his faith; [16] he would undoubtedly have confessed his faith, had he been taken too.

The pitiful condition of the lapsed—the result of general laxity (4-6).

4. These heavenly crowns of the martyrs, these spiritual triumphs of the confessors, [17] these outstanding exploits of our brethren cannot, alas, remove one cause of sorrow: that the Enemy's violence and slaughter has wrought havoc amongst us and has torn away something from our very heart and cast it to the ground. What shall I do, dear brethren, in face of this? My mind tosses this way and that—what shall I say? How shall I say it? Tears and not words can alone express the grief which so deep a wound in our body calls for, which the great gaps in our once

numerous flock evoke from our hearts. Who could be so
callous, so stony-hearted, who so unmindful of brotherly
love, as to remain dry-eyed in the presence of so many of
his own kin who are broken now, shadows of their former
selves, dishevelled, in the trappings of grief? Will he not
burst into tears at sight of them, before finding words for
his sorrow? Believe me, my brothers, I share your distress,
and can find no comfort in my own escape and safety;
for the shepherd feels the wounds of his flock more than
they do. My heart bleeds with each one of you, I share
the weight of your sorrow and distress. I mourn with those
that mourn, I weep with those that weep, with the fallen
I feel I have fallen myself. My limbs too were struck by
the arrows of the lurking foe, his angry sword pierced my
body too. When persecution rages, the mind of none
escapes free and unscathed: when my brethren fell, my
heart was struck and I fell at their side.

5. Yet, dear brethren, we must judge facts as they are,
and the dark clouds of a cruel persecution must not so
blind our eyes that we come to think no light remains to
see what God bids us do. If we know what made us fall,
we can learn how to heal our wounds. The Master
wanted to make trial of His household; and because the
long years of peace had undermined our practice of the
way of life which God had given us, our languid faith—I
had almost said our *sleeping* faith—was now quickened
by the heavenly visitation and, whereas our sins deserved
a punishment still greater, our merciful Lord so tempered
the course of events that what has befallen us seems
rather to have been a testing than a persecution.

6. Each one was intent on adding to his inheritance. Forgetting what the faithful used to do under the Apostles[18]
and[19] what they should always be doing, each one with

insatiable greed was engrossed in increasing his own property. Gone was the devotion of bishops to the service of God, gone was the clergy's[20] faithful integrity, gone the generous compassion for the needy,[21] gone all discipline in our behaviour. Men had their beards plucked,[22] women their faces painted:[23] their eyes must needs be daubed other than God made them, their hair stained a colour not their own. What subtle tricks to deceive the hearts of the simple, what sly manœuvres to entrap the brethren! Marriages contracted with heathens, members of Christ given in prostitution to pagans![24] Not merely imprudent oaths, but perjury itself; swollen pride and contempt for authority; poisonous tongues cursing one another,[25] hatred perpetuating mutual antagonisms. Too many bishops, instead of giving encouragement[26] and example to others, made no account of their being God's ministers, and became the ministers of earthly kings; they left their sees, abandoned their people, and toured the markets in other territories on the lookout for profitable deals. While their brethren in the Church went hungry, they wanted to have money in abundance, they acquired landed estates by fraud, and made profits by loans at compound interest. If that is what we have become, what do we not deserve for such sins, when the judgment of God warned us long since, saying: '*If they forsake my law and walk not in my judgments: if they profane my statutes and observe not my commands: I will visit their crimes with a rod, and their transgressions with scourges*'?[27]

God's commands and warnings forgotten; men even hastened to the sacrifice—dragged others down with them (7–9).
　　7. We had already been told of this and warned beforehand. But heedless of established law and customary

discipline, we brought it upon us by our sins that we should have to face correction for our contempt of God's commands, and should have our faith put to sterner tests; and even then we did not, at long last, come back to the fear of the Lord, so as to bear with courage and patience the punishment and trial which God sent us. At the first threatening words of the Enemy, an all too large number of the brethren betrayed their faith; they were not felled by the violence of the persecution, but fell of their own free will. Was it something unheard-of that had happened, something beyond expectation, that made men recklessly break their oath to Christ,[28] as if a situation had arisen which they had not bargained for? Was it not foretold by the prophets before He came, and by His Apostles since? Were they not inspired by the Holy Spirit to predict that the just would always be oppressed[29] and ill-treated by the gentiles? Was it not to arm our faith at all times, to confirm the servants of God by a voice from heaven that Holy Writ says: *The Lord thy God shalt thou adore, and Him only shalt thou serve?*[30] Was it not to reveal the wrath of the divine displeasure, and to inspire the fear of punishment that it is written: '*They have adored those whom their own hands had made; and man hath bowed himself down, man hath abused himself—and I shall not weaken towards them*';[31] and again God says: '*He that sacrificeth to gods shall be uprooted—save only if to the Lord*'?[32] And in the Gospel later, Our Lord too who taught by word and fulfilled in deed—teaching what was to be, and bringing about what He had foretold—did He not warn us beforehand of all that is now happening and of what shall happen yet? Did He not foreordain eternal pains for those who deny Him, and the reward of salvation for those who confess Him?[33]

8. Oh the scandal of it! Some forgot all this and let it slip their memory. They did not even wait to be arrested before going up [to offer sacrifice];[34] they did not wait to be questioned before they denied their faith. Many were defeated before the battle was joined, they collapsed without any encounter, thus even depriving themselves of the plea that they had sacrificed to the idols against their will. Without any compulsion they hastened to the forum, they hurried of themselves to their death, as if this was what they had long been waiting for, as if they were embracing the opportunity to realize the object of their desires. How many, as night fell, had to be put off till later, and how many even begged the magistrates not to postpone their —doom![35] What pretext of pressure can such men allege to excuse their crime, when it was rather they who pressed for their own destruction? But surely, even if a man did come to the Capitol[36] spontaneously, even if he approached of his own accord to commit himself to this grim crime, did not his step falter, his eyes cloud, did not his heart quake, his limbs tremble? Surely his blood ran cold, his tongue clove to his palate, his speech failed him? Could a servant of God stand there and speak—and renounce Christ, whereas it was the world and the devil he had renounced before? Was not that altar, where he was going to his death, in fact his funeral pyre? When he saw that altar of the devil,[37] smoking and reeking with its foul stench, should he not have fled in terror, as from the place where his soul must burn?[38] Poor fellow, why bring any other offering or victim for the sacrifice? You yourself are the offering and the victim come to the altar; there you have slain your hope of salvation, there in those fatal fires you have reduced your faith to ashes.

9. But many were not content with their own destruction: they encouraged one another and rode to their ruin in a body; with poisoned cup they toasted each other's death! And to crown this accumulation of crimes: parents even carried their babies and led their youngsters to be robbed of what they had received in earliest infancy. When the day of judgment comes, will these not say: 'It was not we who did anything, nor of ourselves that we left Our Lord's food and drink[39] out of eagerness to defile ourselves with those unholy things; it was the wickedness of others which was our ruin—our parents murdered our souls; it was they who in our name denied the Church to be our Mother, and God to be our Father, so that, small and helpless and innocent as we were of so wicked a crime, through their making us join them in their sins, we became the victims of the unscrupulousness of others'?

They could have fled elsewhere, but would not sacrifice their
   possessions (10–12).

10. There is, alas, no sound or serious excuse for so great a crime. A man had only to leave the country and sacrifice his property. Since man is born to die, who is there who must not eventually leave his country and give up his inheritance? It is Christ who must not be left, it is giving up one's salvation and one's eternal home that must be feared. Hear the warning of the Holy Spirit through His prophet: '*Depart ye, depart, go ye out from thence and touch no unclean thing. Go out of the midst of her, break away, you that carry the vessels of the Lord.*'[40] And those who are themselves vessels of the Lord, nay, the temple of God, why do they not go out of the midst and depart, to avoid being compelled to touch the unclean thing, to pollute and

desecrate themselves with poisoned meats? Again, in another place, a voice is heard from heaven warning the servants of God what they should do: '*Go out from her, my people, that thou be not a partaker of her sins, and that thou be not stricken by her plagues.*'[41] The man who goes out and withdraws himself does not partake in her sin, but if he is discovered in sinful association with her, he too will be stricken by the plagues. That is why Our Lord commanded us to withdraw and flee from persecution, and to encourage us to it, He both taught and did so Himself.[42] The crown is bestowed at God's good pleasure and is not received till the appointed hour, so that if a man, abiding in Christ, withdraws[43] for a while, he is not denying his faith but only awaiting the time; but whosoever fell through not departing, showed by staying that he was prepared to deny.

11. My brothers, we must not hide the truth; we must not pass over in silence the true nature of our malady nor its cause. What deceived many was a blind attachment to their patrimony, and if they were not free and ready to take themselves away, it was because their property held them in chains. That is what fettered those who remained, those were the chains which shackled their courage and choked their faith and hampered their judgment and throttled their souls, so that the serpent, whom God had condemned to eat of earth,[44] found in them his food and his prey, because they clung to the things of earth.[45] And Our Lord, the teacher of the good, looking to the future warned us against this, saying: '*If thou wilt be perfect, sell all thou hast and give to the poor, and thou shalt have treasure in heaven: and come follow me.*'[46] If the rich would do this, riches would not be their ruin; if they stored up their treasure in heaven, they would not now have an enemy

and a thief within their own household; their heart and thought and care would be in heaven, if their treasure lay in heaven: no man could be overcome by the world if he had nothing in the world to overcome him. He would follow Our Lord untrammelled and free as the Apostles and many others did at that time,[47] and as some have often done since, leaving their parents and possessions to bind themselves inseparably to Christ.

12. But how can those who are tethered to their inheritance be following Christ? And can those who are weighed down by earthly desires be seeking heaven and aspiring to the heights above? They think of themselves as owners, whereas it is they rather who are owned: enslaved as they are to their own property, they are not the masters of their money but its slaves. The Apostle was pointing to our times and to these very men when he said: *For they that will become rich, fall into temptation and into snares and into many hurtful desires, which drown a man into perdition and destruction. For the desire of money is the root of all evils; which some coveting have erred from the faith, and have entangled themselves in many sorrows.*[48] On the other hand, what rewards does not Our Lord hold out as He invites us to scorn the property we have! For the small, insignificant losses of this world, what rich compensation He makes! 'There is no man,' He says, '*that leaveth house, or land, or parents, or brethren, or wife, or children for the kingdom of God's sake, who shall not receive seven times more in the present time, and in the world to come life everlasting.*'[49] Acknowledging this as we do, and knowing that God is faithful to His promises, not only should we not fear such losses but we should even desire them, for Our Lord Himself has also assured us beforehand: '*Blessed shall you be when they shall persecute you, and when they shall separate*

*you, and when they shall expel you, and shall curse your name
as evil for the Son of man's sake. Be glad in that day and
rejoice: for behold, your reward is great in heaven.*'[50]

*The tortures are no excuse for those who did not undergo them
(13–14).*

13. You will say that tortures came after that, and that
the threat of brutal cruelties hung over those who should
disobey. But a man can only blame the tortures if it is they
that overcame him: the plea of pain can only be made by
one who was broken by the pain. In that case he may well
plead, and say: 'I wanted to do battle bravely; remembering the promise I had sworn,[51] I armed myself with
loyalty and faith, but when engaged in the fight I was
overcome by the repeated tortures and the endlessness of
the suffering. My purpose was firm, my faith strong, and
long did my soul struggle resolutely with the pain of the
tortures. But as the ferocity of the cruel judge flared up
again, I was already exhausted when first I was lashed
with whips, then beaten with truncheons, then stretched
on the rack, then ploughed with hooks, then burnt with
the fire, till I lost heart for the struggle; it was my physical
weakness that gave way, it was not my spirit but my flesh
that cracked under the pain.' Such a plea may truly avail
for forgiveness, such a defence deserves our pity. It was
thus that in this city a short while ago Castus and Aemilius
were pardoned by the Lord; it was thus that, after they
had been worsted in the first engagement, He made them
victors in the second, so that though they had yielded to
the fire before, now they proved themselves the stronger,
and what had then defeated them, now gave them their
victory. They could call on God for pity, not with tears,
but with wounds, not with cries of distress, but with the

sufferings of their tortured limbs; in place of tears it was their blood that flowed, in place of weeping the blood streamed from their deep-seared flesh.[51a]

14. But what wounds can be shown here by the vanquished, what cuts in gaping flesh, what crippling of their limbs, when it was not faith that fell in the fight, but loss of faith that forestalled the fight? The fallen has not the excuse that he was forced to the crime when the crime was his own choice. I am not saying this to add to the load of my brethren's guilt: rather is it to spur them on to the prayer of reparation.[52] For since it is written: *They that call you blessed are leading you into error and confusing the path of your feet,*[53] he who soothes the sinner with comforting flatteries only encourages the sinful appetite; he is not checking crime but fostering it. But he whose advice is more vigorous, administering rebuke and instruction at once, is setting his brother on the way of salvation. '*Such as I love,*' saith the Lord, '*I upbraid and chastise.*'[54] Therefore, the duty of a bishop of the Lord is, not to deceive with false flatteries, but to provide the remedies needed for salvation. He is a poor doctor whose timid hand spares the swelling, festering wound, and who, by letting the poison remain buried deep in the body, only aggravates the ill. The wound must be cut open, the infected parts[55] cut out, and the wound treated with stringent remedies. Let the patient shout and cry never so much, let him protest in exasperation at the pain—later he will be grateful, when he feels his health restored.

The lapsed need to do penance: they must not be deceived by offers of easy reconciliation (15–17).

15. For, dear brethren, there has now appeared a new source of disaster[56] and, as if the fierce storm of persecu-

tion had not been enough, there has come to crown it a subtle evil, an innocent-seeming pestilence, which masquerades as compassion.[57] Contrary to the full strength of the Gospel, contrary to the law of Our Lord and God, through certain people's[58] presumption a deceptive readmission to communion is being granted,[59] a reconciliation that is null and void, one that imperils the givers and is worthless to those who receive it.[60] The latter no longer seek the slow painful road to recovery, nor the genuine cure through satisfaction done; what remorse they had has been snatched from their breasts, the gravity and enormity of their crime has been blotted from their memory. The wounds they are dying of are covered up and, through pretence of lack of pain, the mortal affection deep in their organism is concealed. People coming back from the altars of Satan approach Our Lord's sacred body,[61] their hands still foul and reeking;[62] while still belching, one may say, from the poisonous food of the idols—their breath even yet charged with the foulness of their crime and with the stench of their repulsive death-feast—they desecrate the body of the Lord, whereas Sacred Scripture cries aloud against them: *He that is clean shall eat of the flesh, and if any man shall eat of the flesh of the saving sacrifice which is the Lord's, and his own defilement be upon him, that man shall perish from among his people.*[63] So the Apostle also testifies when he says: *You cannot drink the chalice of the Lord and the chalice of devils; you cannot have communion at the table of the Lord and at the table of devils;*[64] and he threatens and denounces the obstinate and the unrighteous, saying: *Whosoever shall eat the bread and drink the chalice of the Lord unworthily shall be guilty of the body and of the blood of the Lord.*[65]

16. With utter neglect and contempt for all this,

without making any expiation for their sins or any open acknowledgment[66] of their guilt, before their conscience has been purified by any sacrifice offered by the priest or by imposition of hands,[67] before the menacing anger of their offended Lord has been appeased, they make an assault upon His body and blood, and their hands and mouth sin more grievously now against their Lord than when with their lips they denied Him. They think that it is the *pax*[68] which certain men[69] are hawking about[70] with honeyed words; it is not peace but war, and no one is in union with the Church who cuts himself off from the Gospel. Why do those men describe the harm they inflict as a blessing? Why do they call the sacrilege they commit a sacrament?[71] Why do they admit to communion, as they pretend, those who should still be weeping and calling on God's mercy, making them drop all sorrowing and penance?

Those men do as much harm to the lapsed as hail to the crops, as a wild tempest does to trees; they are like a ravening plague to cattle, like a fierce storm to ships at sea. They rob men of the comfort of hope, they tear them up by the roots, their poisonous words spread a deadly contagion, they dash the ship against the rocks to prevent its making port. Their indulgence does not mean the granting of reconciliation but its frustration, it does not restore men to communion but bars them from it and from salvation.[72] This is a new sort of persecution, a new sort of temptation, by which the crafty Enemy[73] still attacks the lapsed, and ranges about wreaking unsuspected devastation: silencing lamentation, dispensing from repentance, abolishing all memory of crime; no breast is to sigh, no tears to flow, no long, expiatory penance is to implore the mercy of a Lord so grievously offended. Yet is it written: '*Remember from whence thou art fallen: and do penance.*'[74]

17. Let no man deceive himself, let none be misled. Only the Lord can grant mercy.[75] Sins committed against Him can be cancelled[76] by Him alone who bore our sins and suffered for us, by Him whom God delivered up for our sins. Man cannot be above God,[77] nor can the servant by any indulgence of his own remit or condone the graver sort of crime committed against his Lord, for that would make the lapsed liable to this further charge, that he knows not[78] the words of the prophet: '*Cursed be the man that putteth his hope in man.*'[79] It is Our Lord we must pray to,[80] it is Our Lord we must win over by our satisfaction; for He has said He will deny the man that denies Him,[81] and He alone has received all power of judgment from His Father.[82]

The intercession of the martyrs has its own virtue: but not against the Gospel (17–20).

We do not call in question the power which the merits of the martyrs[83] and the works of the just have with the Judge, but that will be when the day of judgment comes, when after the passing of this present world,[84] Christ's flock stands before His tribunal. 18. If, however, anyone[85] in his impatience of delay thinks that he can condone the sins of all, presuming thus to override Our Lord's commands,[85a] so far from benefiting the lapsed his rashness does them harm. To disregard His decree[86] is to call down His anger, if one thinks that there is no need now to appeal to His mercy, but, treating the Lord with contempt, one presumes to exercise indulgence oneself. At the foot of God's altar[87] the souls of the martyrs who have been slain cry aloud saying: *How long, O Lord, holy and true, dost*

Thou not judge and revenge our blood on them that dwell on the earth?[88] And they are told that they must wait and have patience yet awhile. Is it credible, then,[89] that anyone should wish for good to be done, by wholesale remissions and condonations of sin, *against* the will of the Judge, or that before he has himself been avenged, he should have the power to defend others? Suppose[90] the martyrs do want something done; if it is good and lawful, if it does not involve that God's bishop should act against Our Lord Himself, then let him accede readily and with all deference to their wishes—provided of course that the petitioner observes a becoming modesty. The martyrs want something done, no doubt; but if their behest is not in the Lord's written Law, we must first know whether what they ask for has been granted to them by the Lord, and only then carry out their bidding.[91] We cannot take it for granted that because man has made a promise, the same has been granted by the majesty of God.

19. For even Moses prayed on behalf of the sins of the people without securing pardon for the sinners he was pleading for. *I beseech Thee, Lord,* he said, *this people hath committed a grievous crime; . . . and now if Thou wouldst forgive them their crime, forgive them; but if not, strike me out of the book that Thou hast written. And the Lord said to Moses: 'If a man hath sinned before me, him will I strike out of my book.'*[92] Moses was the friend of God, Moses had often spoken with the Lord face to face, yet he was unable to obtain what he asked for, and his intercession did not appease God's offended anger. Jeremias was praised and extolled by God: *'Before I formed thee in the bowels of thy mother, I knew thee, and before thou camest forth out of the womb, I sanctified thee and appointed thee a prophet unto the nations,'*[93] and yet when he besought and prayed repeatedly

for the sins of the people, God said to him: '*Pray not for this people, and ask not for them in prayer and petition; for I will not hear them in the time when they shall call upon me, in the time of their affliction.*'[94] Again, was ever justice greater than Noe's, who when the world was covered with sins, was the only just man found on earth? Was ever glory greater than Daniel's? In enduring martyrdoms was there ever constancy in the faith[95] more robust than his, or more favour of God enjoyed, who so often was put to the test and won; and winning, survived unscathed?[95a] Was there ever alacrity in service greater than Job's, greater fortitude in trials, greater patience in suffering, greater resignation in time of fear, greater staunchness of faith than his? And yet God said that not even if *they* were to ask, would He grant their prayer. When the prophet Ezechiel was praying for his sinful people, God spoke: '*Whatever land shall sin against me so as to commit iniquity, I will stretch forth my hand upon it and will destroy its support of bread, and I will send famine upon it and will carry off man and beast from it. Even if these three men, Noe, Daniel, and Job, shall be in it, . . . they shall deliver neither sons nor daughters, but they themselves alone shall be saved.*'[96] So true is it that not every request is settled by the merits of the petitioner, but that it lies at the discretion of the giver,[97] and no human verdict can presume to claim any authority, unless God's judgment concurs.

20. In the Gospel, Our Lord says: '*He that shall confess me before men, I will also confess him before my Father who is in heaven; but he that shall deny me, I will also deny him.*'[98] If He is not to deny the man who denies Him,[99] neither will He confess him who confesses Him; the Gospel cannot in part stand and in part fail: either both parts must hold, or both must lose their authority. If those who deny Him

are not to be held guilty of a crime, neither shall those who confess Him receive[100] the reward of virtue. But if the victory of faith receives its crown, the defeat of faithlessness must receive its punishment. Therefore, either the martyrs avail nothing, if the Gospel fails; or, if the Gospel cannot fail, then those whom the Gospel enables to become martyrs, cannot act in opposition to the Gospel. But let none, my dear brethren, let none besmirch the fair name of the martyrs, let none rob them of the glory of their crown. The strength and purity of their faith stands unimpaired: nothing can be said or done against Christ by one whose whole hope and faith, whose whole strength and glory abides in Christ; those who themselves have fulfilled the commands of God, cannot instigate the bishops to act against the command of God.[101]

God's judgments provoked by sin and insubordination; some recent instances of prompt retribution (20–26).

Or[102] does some individual think himself greater than God or more merciful than the divine goodness, that he should want to undo what God has allowed to take place and, as if God were unequal to the protection of His Church, should pretend to come to our rescue and save us? 21. Or was it, perhaps,[103] without God's knowledge that these things happened, or without His permission that all these calamities[104] befell us? Let the stubborn[105] learn, and the forgetful be reminded what Sacred Scripture says: *Who hath given Jacob for a spoil, and Israel to those who were pillaging him? Is it not God, He against whom they have sinned refusing to walk in His ways or hearken to His Law? And He drew down upon them the fury of His wrath.*[106] And elsewhere it testifies thus: *Has then the hand of God lost its power that it cannot save, or has He dulled His ear that it cannot hear? But your sins form a barrier between you and your God, and because of your sins He turns His face from you lest He have mercy.*[107] Let us reckon up our sins, let us examine the secret springs of our actions and desires, and ponder what in conscience we deserve. Let us recognize in our hearts that we have not walked in the ways of the Lord, that we have cast aside the Law of God, that we have never been willing to obey[108] His commands and salutary warnings.

22. What good can there be in a man, what can you think of his fear of the Lord or of his faith, when neither warnings have been able to correct him, nor even persecution has induced him to reform? His stiff and arrogant neck was not bowed even by his fall; his proud and swollen spirit was not quelled even by defeat. Stricken to the dust, he challenges those who are standing unscathed; and because Our Lord's body is not at once placed in his unclean hands nor his polluted mouth given Our Lord's blood to drink, he raves against the sacred ministers— steeped in sacrilege as he is.[109] Yes, you rave—and what madness could be greater? You rave against him who is trying to shield you from the anger of God, you abuse him who invokes Our Lord's mercy upon you, who feels your wound as his own which you do not feel yourself; who weeps for you who, it seems, weep not for yourself. You are only heaping up and adding to your guilt, and if you pursue the bishops and priests of God[110] so unrelentingly, do you think that Our Lord will be moved to relent[111] towards you?

23. No—hear what we say and take it to heart. Why are your ears deaf to the rules of salvation that we propose? Why are your eyes blind to the road of penitence that we point to? Why is your mind closed and prejudiced in the

presence of the life-giving remedies which we learn and proclaim from the Holy Scriptures? If certain doubters have too little faith in what the future holds in store, let them learn to tremble from what is happening even now. Look at what penalties we see overtaking men who have denied the faith, what an evil end, alas! they have come to. Not even here below can they go unpunished, though the day of reckoning is yet to come. If some are struck down already,[112] it is to instruct the rest. The penalty of a few[113] is a warning to all.

24. Among those who of their own accord went up to the Capitol[114] to deny Christ, there was one who after his denial was struck dumb. His punishment fell where his crime had begun; now he could not even pray, as he had no words with which to beg for mercy.[115] Another, a woman, went to the baths—as she had lost the grace of the waters of baptism, her sin and sorry state wanted nothing but she must make straight for the baths, of all places![115a] But there, unclean as she was, she was possessed by an unclean spirit, and with her teeth she bit her own tongue to pieces because it had tasted and uttered[116] such impious things. The criminal food had filled her mouth with such rage as to become a weapon for her own destruction. She was made her own executioner and could not long survive: in the throes of internal pangs she expired.

25. Listen to what happened in my presence, before my very eyes. There was a baby girl, whose parents had fled and had, in their fear, rather improvidently left it in the charge of its nurse. The nurse took the helpless child to the magistrates. There, before the idol where the crowds were flocking, as it was too young to eat the flesh, they gave it some bread dipped in what was left of the wine offered by those who had already doomed themselves.[117]

Later, the mother recovered her child. But the girl could not reveal or tell the wicked thing that had been done, any more than she had been able to understand or ward it off before. Thus, when the mother brought her in with her while we were offering the Sacrifice,[118] it was through ignorance that this mischance occurred.[119] But the infant, in the midst of the faithful,[120] resenting the prayer and the offering[121] we were making, began to cry convulsively,[122] struggling and tossing in a veritable brain-storm, and for all its tender age and simplicity of soul, was confessing, as if under torture, in every way it could, its consciousness of the misdeed. Moreover, when the sacred rites[123] were completed and the deacon began ministering to those present,[124] when its turn came to receive, it turned its little head away as if sensing the divine presence, it closed its mouth, held its lips tight, and refused to drink from the chalice.[125] The deacon persisted and, in spite of its opposition, poured in some of the consecrated chalice. There followed choking and vomiting. The Eucharist could not remain in a body or a mouth that was defiled; the drink which had been sanctified by Our Lord's blood[126] returned from the polluted stomach. So great is the power of the Lord, so sacred His majesty; under His light the hidden corners of darkness were laid bare, even secret crimes did not escape the priest of God.[127]

26. So much for the child involved in the crime of others, but too young to reveal it. But an older girl, already growing up, slipped in secretly among those assisting at [our] sacrifice.[128] It was not food that she took so much as a sword against herself, and what she swallowed might have been some deadly poison entering her breast. After the first spasms, struggling for breath, she began to choke and, a victim now not of the persecution but of her own

crime, she collapsed in tremors and convulsions. The guilt which she had tried to hide did not remain long unpunished or concealed. If she had deceived man, she was made to feel the avenging hand of God.

There was a woman too who with impure hands tried to open the locket[129] in which she was keeping Our Lord's holy body,[130] but fire flared up from it and she was too terrified to touch it. And a man who, in spite of his sin, also presumed secretly to join the rest in receiving of the sacrifice[131] offered by the bishop,[132] was unable to eat or even handle Our Lord's sacred body; when he opened his hands, he found he was holding nothing but ashes. By this one example it was made manifest that Our Lord removes Himself from one who denies Him, and that what is received brings no blessing[133] to the unworthy, since the Holy One[134] has fled and the saving grace is turned to ashes.

How many there are every day who, refusing to do penance or to confess the guilt on their souls,[135] become possessed by unclean spirits, how many are driven out of their senses in a frenzy of fury and madness! No need to recount the fate of each, since among the innumerable calamities in the world, the variety of the punishments is as great as the number of the sinners themselves. Let each one consider not what has befallen someone else but what affliction he deserves himself; and let him not think that he has escaped because no penalty has yet overtaken him; he has all the more to fear if the wrath of the divine Judge has reserved him for itself.

Those who only secured certificates of sacrifice sinned less grievously, yet their guilt is great (27–28).

27. Nor let people flatter themselves that they need do

no penance because they have kept their hands clean from the accursed sacrifices, when all the time they have certificates of sacrifice on their conscience. Why, such a certificate is itself a confession of apostasy,[135a] it is a testimonial that the Christian has renounced what he once was. All that others have done in fact, he says he has done too; and in view of the Scripture saying: '*Ye cannot serve two masters,*'[136] he has served an earthly master, he has obeyed his decree, he has obeyed a man's command rather than God's. Small comfort to him that the publication of 'what he did' has saved his honour and reputation a little in the eyes of men;[137] he will not be able to escape the eye of God his Judge, for the Holy Spirit says in the Psalms: *Thy eyes have seen what is the imperfection of my being, and in Thy book all shall be written;*[138] and again: *Man looks upon the countenance, but God upon the heart;*[139] and the Lord Himself forewarns and forearms us: '*And all the churches shall know that I am the searcher of the reins and the heart.*'[140] He sees what is secret and hidden, He discerns what is concealed, and no man can evade the eyes of the God who says: '*I am a God at hand, and not a God afar. If a man be hid in secret places, shall I not therefore see Him?*'[141] He sees the heart and conscience of every man, and He who is to judge not only our deeds, but also our words and thoughts, contemplates the movements of the minds and wills of all, hidden though they be in the recesses of the soul.

28. And lastly, how much greater is the faith and more salutary the fear of those who, though bound by no crime of sacrifice or certificate, yet merely because they entertained such a thought, confess even this to the priests of God simply and contritely, and manifest their conscience[142] to them. They lay bare the burden that is on their minds

and seek treatment for their wounds, light and superficial as they are, knowing that it is written: *God is not mocked*.[143] God cannot be mocked or outwitted, no clever cunning can deceive Him. Indeed, a man sins all the more grievously if he judges of God by human standards and thinks he will escape the penalty of his sin because he committed no overt act. Christ in His teaching says: '*He that shall be ashamed of me . . . him shall the Son of man put to shame*';[143a] and can a man account himself a Christian if being a Christian makes him blush and[144] afraid to admit it? How can he be 'with Christ' if he is ashamed and afraid to belong to Christ? Let us grant that he has sinned the less because he avoided looking upon the idols and profaning the sanctity of his faith before the eyes of a scoffing multitude, and because he avoided polluting his hands with the offerings of perdition and befouling his mouth with the execrable food: his only gain is that his guilt is less, not that his conscience is free from stain. More easily can he obtain pardon for his sin, but guilty he is for all that; let him persevere in doing penance and imploring God's mercy, lest what made for the mitigation of his crime turn to its increase through the neglect of reparation.[145]

Genuine penance is called for, after the example of the Saints of the Old Law (29-32).

29. Let each one, I entreat you, brethren, confess his sin while he who has sinned is still in this world, while his confession[146] can still be heard, while satisfaction and forgiveness granted through the priests[147] are pleasing to God. Let us turn back to the Lord with our whole heart and, expressing our repentance in deep sorrow, implore God for His mercy. Let our souls bow before Him, let our sorrow be offered to Him in satisfaction, let our hopes all

rest in Him. He Himself has told us how to ask: '*Return to me from all your heart, along with fasting and weeping and mourning, and rend your hearts and not your garments.*'[148] Let us return to the Lord with all our hearts, let us appease His anger and displeasure, by fasting, tears, and lamentations, as He Himself enjoins.

30. But are we to believe that a man is sorrowing with all his heart, that he is calling on the Lord with fasting, tears, and lamentations, when from the very day of his sin he is found daily at the baths,[148a] or after feasting sumptuously and gorging himself to excess he is next day belching with indigestion, and never shares any of his food or drink with those in need?[149] When he goes about laughing cheerfully, how can he be lamenting the state of death he is in? And whereas it is written: '*You shall not spoil the appearance of your beards,*'[150] why is he plucking hairs from his beard and making up his face? Is he courting someone's favour when he is out of favour with God? Or is that lady sighing and sorrowing who spends her time decking herself out in rich dresses, without a thought for the 'putting on of Christ'[151] which she has lost; or when she dons such costly ornaments and jewelled necklaces, without a sigh for the lost splendour of holiness with which God once decked her? For all the foreign garments you put on, for all your silks from China—you are naked still; with whatever gold and pearls and jewels you enhance your beauty, without Christ's beauty you are unsightly still. Dye your hair no more, at least now that you are in mourning; and as for your eyes which you paint up with kohl, let tears, at least now, wash them clean of it.[152] If death had robbed you of one of your dear ones, you would mourn and weep in sorrow; with face neglected, finery laid aside, hair dishevelled, melancholy look and eyes cast down, you would

show every sign of grief. Yet now, for shame, when you have lost your very soul and only survive here in a life of spiritual death, walking about in your own corpse—why are you not weeping bitterly and moaning inconsolably? Why do you not hide away, out of shame for your crime, and give yourself up to your grief? Nay, your wounds are even greater, your guilt still deeper: for after sinning you make no atonement, you have fallen and you do not repent.

31. Those noble and splendid youths, Ananias, Azarias, and Misael, even in the flaming heat of the fiery furnace ceased not making confession to God.[153] Though they were clear in conscience, having often earned God's favour[154] by the service of their faith and reverence, yet they persevered in humility and in making satisfaction to God even in the midst of those tortures[155] which so gloriously testified to their virtues. Holy Scripture records that: *standing, Azarias prayed and opened his mouth and made confession to God together with his companions in the midst of the fire.*[156] Daniel too, even after the many graces which rewarded his faith and innocence, after being repeatedly honoured by the Lord for his virtues and merits, yet continued to strive after God's favour and, rolling on the ground in sackcloth and ashes, made his confession in sorrow, saying: *O Lord God, the great and the strong and the terrible, who keepest the covenant and mercy to them that love Thee and keep Thy commandments, we have sinned, we have transgressed and abandoned Thy commands and Thy judgments. We have not listened to what Thy children the Prophets have spoken in Thy name over our kings and all the nations and over all the earth. To Thee, O Lord, to Thee be justice, but to us distress.*[157]

32. This is what those who were meek and simple and

innocent did to win the favour of the majesty of God; and to-day those who have even denied the Lord refuse to pray to the Lord or to make satisfaction! Brethren, submit, I beg you, to the remedies of salvation; yield to better counsels, join your tears to ours, add your sorrow to our sorrow.[158] We appeal to you, so as to be able to appeal to the Lord for you; to you first we direct the prayers which we are offering to God for you, that He may show you mercy. Carry out your penance to the full, show proof of the sorrow of a repentant and contrite heart.

Avoid the example and the company of unrepentant sinners and their abettors (33–34).

33. And do not be influenced by the recklessness or silly empty-headedness of certain folk who, for all the gravity of their guilt, are so blinded in soul that they neither recognize their sins nor repent of them. Thus has God's anger struck them a still greater blow, as it is written: *And God has stricken their minds through;*[159] and again: *They received not the love of the truth, that they might be saved. And therefore God shall send them the operation of error, to believe lying: that all may be judged who have not believed the truth but are contented in their injustice.*[160] Thus, self-contented without justice, their minds stricken with a foolish madness, they despise the commands of God, they leave their wounds untended, they refuse to do penance. Reckless before their fall, they are without remorse after it; weak-kneed before, they kneel not after; when they should have stood firm, they fell, when they should throw themselves prostrate before God, they think themselves to stand.[161] None gave them reconciliation,[162] they presumed it for themselves; they have yielded to false promises and, joining apostates and renegades, they are receiving a sham

in place of the reality, taking as valid the communion of
those who are themselves not in communion; they are
putting their faith in men in despite of God,[163] after failing
to profess their faith in God in despite of men.[164]

34. Do all you can to break away from such men; as you
value your salvation, avoid those who associate with such
harmful connections. Their talk spreads like a canker,[165]
their conversation is as catching[166] as an infection, their
poisonous and pernicious propaganda is more deadly than
was the persecution itself. The latter leaves the door open
to penance and satisfaction; but those who do away with
penance for sin, shut the door against satisfaction altogether. And so it is that, through the presumption of
certain folk who beguile with false promises of salvation,
all true hope of salvation is destroyed.

Implore God's mercy by penance and almsdeeds: He is kind and
full of mercy, He will strengthen and reward (35–36).

35. But those among you, my brothers, who are respon-
sive to the fear of God and who despite your fall are
conscious of your plight, let the sight of your sins move
you to penance and sorrow; acknowledge how grievously
your conscience reproaches you, open your soul to the
realization of your crime, neither despairing of God's
mercy nor yet claiming instant pardon. While God in His
fatherly affection is ever forgiving and kind, in His majesty
as Judge, He deserves our fear. Let the earnestness of our
repentance correspond to the gravity of our sin. When the
wound is so serious, let it have the exacting and prolonged
treatment it needs; let the penance do full justice to the
crime. Do you think that God will be appeased[167] in a
moment—God, whom you repudiated with treasonable
words; God, whom you chose to place lower than your

patrimony; God, whose temple you polluted with the defilement of sacrilege?[168] Do you think that He will easily have mercy on you,[169] after your saying that He meant nothing to you?

You must beg and pray assiduously, spend the day sorrowing and the night in vigils and tears, fill every moment with weeping and lamentation; you must lie on the ground amidst clinging ashes, toss about chafing in the sackcloth of mourning; having once been clothed with Christ, refuse all other raiment now; having supped with the devil, choose rather now to fast; apply yourself to good deeds[170] which can wash away your sins, be constant and generous in giving alms, whereby souls are freed from death. What the Adversary was trying to make his own, let it become Christ's. A man should not keep and love that patrimony which ensnared him and caused his downfall. Such property must be shunned like an enemy, fled from like a highwayman; those who own it must fear it as they would fear poison or the sword. Let what remains of it serve only to make reparation for the guilt of sin. Let your largess be without delay, without stint,[171] let all your wealth be expended on the healing of your wound; let us use our goods and our riches to make Our Lord beholden to us,[172] for He is one day to be our Judge. Such was the rich fruit of faith in the Apostles' time, this was how the first assembly of believers observed Christ's commands: they gave at once, and generously. They gave their all to be distributed by the Apostles—yet[173] they had no such crimes to repair.

36. To him who prays with all his heart, to him who mourns with tears and sighs of true repentance, to him who by good works of persevering charity pleads to the Lord for mercy on his sin—to such He can extend His

mercy,[174] since He has shown the mercy of His heart when He said:[175] '*When you return and mourn, then shall you be saved and know where you once were*';[176] and again: '*I desire not the death of the dying,' saith the Lord, 'but that he return and live.*'[177] And the prophet Joel, at the bidding of the Lord, declares the Lord's loving-kindness: *Return*, he says, *to the Lord your God, for He is merciful and kind and patient and full of mercy and ready to revoke His sentence upon wicked deeds.*[178] He can be indulgent; He can revoke His own condemnation. Towards sorrow, good works, pleadings, He can show clemency and forgive; He can take into account what the martyrs have asked for on their behalf and what the bishops have done for them.[179] Nay, when a man's reparation is such as to touch His heart still more, when the sincerity of his pleading appeases His anger at the offence, He equips the vanquished with arms once more, and restores and reinforces the vitality whereby faith is renewed and can bear fruit. A soldier once more he will return to the fray, he will engage anew and challenge the enemy—and will do so with all the more zest for his remorse. He who has made such satisfaction to God, he who by his repentance and shame for his sin, draws from the bitterness of his fall[180] a fresh fund of valour and loyalty, shall by the help he has won from the Lord, rejoice the heart of the Church whom he has so lately pained; he will earn not merely God's forgiveness, but His crown.

THE UNITY OF THE CATHOLIC CHURCH

The devil's wiles must be unmasked and overcome by obedience to Christ's commands (1-2).

1. Our Lord solemnly warns us: '*You are the salt of the earth*,'[1] and bids us in our love of good to be not only simple but prudent as well. Accordingly, dearest brethren, what else ought we to do but be on our guard and watch vigilantly, in order to know the snares of our crafty foe and to avoid them?[2] Otherwise, after putting on Christ who is the Wisdom of God the Father,[3] we may be found to have failed in wisdom for the care of our souls.[4] It is not persecution alone that we ought to fear, nor those forces that in open warfare range abroad to overthrow and defeat the servants of God. It is easy enough to be on one's guard when the danger is obvious; one can stir up one's courage for the fight when the Enemy shows himself in his true colours. There is more need to fear and beware of the Enemy when he creeps up secretly,[5] when he beguiles us by a show of peace and steals forward by those hidden approaches which have earned him the name of the 'Serpent.' Such is ever his craft: lurking in the dark, he ensnares men by trickery. That was how at the very beginning of the world he deceived and by lying words of flattery beguiled the unguarded credulity of a simple soul; that was how he tried to tempt Our Lord Himself, approaching Him in disguise, as though he could once more creep upon his victim and deceive Him. But he was recognized and beaten back, and he was defeated precisely through being detected and unmasked.

2. Here we are given an example how to break company with the 'old man,'[6] how to follow in the steps of Christ to victory, so that we may not carelessly stumble again into the snare of death, but being alive to the danger, hold fast to the immortality given us. And how can we hold fast to immortality unless we observe those commandments of Christ by which death is defeated and conquered? He Himself assures us: *'If thou wilt attain to life, keep the commandments'*;[7] and again: *'If ye do what I command you, I call you no longer servants but friends.'*[8] He says that it is those who so act[9] that are strong and firm; it is *they* that are founded in massive security upon a rock,[10] *they* that are established in unshakable solidity, proof against all the storms and hurricanes of the world. *'Him that heareth my words and doeth them,'* He says, *'I will liken to the wise man who built his house upon the rock. The rain fell, the floods rose, the winds came and they crashed against that house: but it fell not. For it was founded upon the rock.'*[11]

We must therefore carry out His words: whatsoever He taught and did, that must we learn and do ourselves. Indeed how can a man say he believes in Christ if he does not do what Christ commanded him to do? Or how shall a man who when under command will not keep faith,[12] hope to receive the reward of faith? He who does not keep to the true way of salvation[13] will inevitably falter and stray; caught up by some gust of error, he will be tossed about like windswept dust; walk as he may, he will make no advance towards his salvation.

In face of heresy and schism, we must recognize that Christ founded the Church on Peter. Expansion no detriment to oneness (3–5).

3. However, we must not only beware of all that is

obvious and unmistakable, but also of all that can deceive
by fraud and cunning. What could be more clever and
cunning than the Enemy's moves after being unmasked
and worsted by Christ's coming?[14] Light had come to the
gentiles and the lamp of salvation was shining for the
deliverance[15] of mankind, so that the deaf began to
hearken to the Spirit's call of grace, the blind to open their
eyes upon the Lord, the sick to recover their health unto
eternity, the lame to make speed to the Church, and the
dumb to raise their voice aloud in prayer. Thereupon the
Enemy, seeing his idols abandoned and his temples and
haunts deserted by the ever growing numbers of the faithful, devised a fresh deceit, using the Christian name itself[16]
to mislead the unwary. He invented heresies and schisms
so as to undermine the faith, to corrupt the truth, to sunder
our unity.[17] Those whom he has failed to keep in the
blindness of their old ways he beguiles, and leads them up
a new road of illusion. He snatches away people from
within the Church herself, and while they think that
coming close to the light they have now done with the
night of the world, he plunges them unexpectedly into
darkness of another kind.[18] They still call themselves
Christians after abandoning the Gospel of Christ and the
observance of His law;[19] though walking in darkness they
think they still enjoy the light. The Enemy cajoles and
deceives them; as the Apostle says, he transforms himself
into an angel of light, and primes his servants to act as the
servants of justice,[20] to call the night day, and damnation
salvation, to teach recklessness under the pretext of hope,[20a]
disbelief under colour of the faith, Antichrist under the
name of Christ, so that by lies that have all the appearance
of truth, they undermine the truth with trickery. All this
has come about, dearest brethren, because men do not go

back to the origin of [the Christian] realities,[21] because they do not look for their source, nor keep to the teaching of their heavenly Master.[22]

4. But if anyone considers those things carefully, he will need no long discourse or arguments. The proof is simple and convincing, being summed up in a matter of fact.[23] The Lord says to Peter:[24] '*I say to thee, that thou art Peter and upon this rock I will build my Church, and the gates of hell shall not overcome it. I will give to thee the keys of the kingdom of heaven. And what thou shalt bind upon earth shall be bound also in heaven, and whatsoever thou shalt loose on earth shall be loosed also in heaven.*'[25]

[1st edition]

And He says to him again after the resurrection: '*Feed my sheep.*'[25a] It is on him that He builds the Church, and to him that He entrusts the sheep to feed. And although He assigns a like power to all the Apostles,[26] yet He founded a single Chair, thus establishing by His own authority the source and hallmark of the [Church's] oneness.[27] No doubt the others were all that Peter was, but a primacy is given to Peter,[28] and it is [thus] made clear that there is but one Church and one Chair. So too, even if they are all shepherds, we are shown but one flock which is to be fed by all the Apostles in common accord. If a man does not hold fast to

[2nd edition]

It is on one man[31] that He builds the Church, and although He assigns a like power to all the Apostles after His resurrection, saying: '*As the Father hath sent me, I also send you. . . . Receive ye the Holy Spirit: if you forgive any man his sins, they shall be forgiven him; if you retain any man's, they shall be retained,*'[32] yet, in order that the oneness might be unmistakable, He established by His own authority a source for that oneness having its origin in one man alone. No doubt the other Apostles were all that Peter was, endowed with equal dignity and power, but the start comes from him alone, in order to show that the Church of Christ is unique.[33]

this oneness of Peter,[29] does he imagine that he still holds the faith? If he deserts the Chair of Peter[30] upon whom the Church was built, has he still confidence that he is in the Church?

Indeed this oneness of the Church is figured in the Canticle of Canticles when the Holy Spirit, speaking in Our Lord's name, says: '*One is my dove, my perfect one: to her mother she is the only one, the darling of her womb.*'[34] If a man does not hold fast to this oneness of the Church, does he imagine that he still holds the faith? If he resists and withstands the Church, has he still confidence that he is in the Church, when the blessed Apostle Paul[35] gives us this very teaching and points to the mystery of Oneness[36] saying: '*One body and one Spirit, one hope of your calling, one Lord, one Faith, one Baptism, one God*'?[37]

5.

5. Now this oneness we must hold to[38] firmly and insist on—especially we who are bishops[39] and exercise authority in the Church—so as to demonstrate[40] that the episcopal power is one and undivided too. Let none mislead the brethren with a lie, let none corrupt the true content of the faith[41] by a faithless perversion of the truth.

The authority of the bishops forms a unity,[42] of which each holds his part in its totality.[43] And the Church forms a unity, however far she spreads and multiplies by the progeny of her fecundity; just as the sun's rays are many, yet the light is one, and a tree's branches are many, yet the strength deriving from its sturdy root is one. So too, though many streams flow from a single spring, though its multiplicity seems scattered abroad by the copiousness of its welling waters,[44] yet their oneness abides by reason of their starting point.[45] Cut off one of the sun's rays—the unity of that body permits no [such] division of its light;[46] break off a branch from the tree, it can bud no more; dam off a stream from its source, it dries up below the cut. So too Our Lord's Church is radiant with light and pours her rays over the whole world; but it is one and the same light which is spread everywhere, and the unity of her body suffers no division. She spreads her branches in generous growth over all the earth, she extends her abundant streams ever further; yet one is the head-spring, one the source, one the mother who is prolific in her offspring, generation after generation: of her womb are we born, of her milk are we fed, of her Spirit our souls draw their life-breath.

Scriptural types of the oneness and indivisibility of the Church (6–9).

6. The spouse of Christ[47] cannot be defiled, she is inviolate and chaste; she knows one home alone, in all modesty she keeps faithfully to one only couch. It is she who rescues us for God, she who seals[47a] for the kingdom the sons whom she has borne. Whoever breaks with the Church and enters on an adulterous union, cuts himself off from the promises made to the Church; and he who has turned his back on the Church of Christ shall not come to the rewards of Christ: he is an alien, a worldling, an enemy. You cannot have God for your Father if you have

not the Church for your mother.[48] If there was escape for anyone who was outside the ark of Noe,[49] there is escape too for one who is found to be outside the Church.[50] Our Lord warns us when He says: *'He that is not with me is against me, and he that gathereth not with me, scattereth.'*[51] Whoever breaks the peace and harmony of Christ acts against Christ; whoever gathers elsewhere than in the Church, scatters the Church of Christ. Our Lord says: *'I and the Father are One'*;[52] and again, of Father, Son, and Holy Spirit it is written: *And the three are One.*[53] Does anyone think then that this oneness, which derives from the stability of God[54] and is welded together after the celestial pattern,[55] can be sundered in the Church and divided by the clash of discordant wills? If a man does not keep this unity,[56] he is not keeping the law of God; he has lost his faith about Father and Son, he has lost his life and his soul.

7. This holy mystery of oneness,[57] this unbreakable bond of close-knit harmony is portrayed in the Gospel by Our Lord Jesus Christ's coat, which was not divided or cut at all, but when they drew lots[58] for the vesture of Christ to see which of them should put on Christ, it was the whole coat that was won, the garment was acquired unspoiled and undivided. These are the words of Holy Scripture: *Now as to His coat, because it was from the upper part woven throughout without a seam, they said to one another: Let us not divide it, but let us cast lots for it, whose it shall be.*[59] The 'oneness' with which He was clothed[60] came 'from the upper part,' that is, from His Father in heaven, and could in no way be divided by any who came to acquire it: it retained its well-knit wholeness indivisibly. That man cannot possess the garment of Christ who rends and divides the Church of Christ. For this reason,

by contrast,[61] when Solomon was dying and his kingdom and people were to be divided, Achias the prophet on meeting king Jeroboam in the field tore his own garment into twelve pieces saying: *Take to thyself ten pieces, for thus saith the Lord: 'Behold I rend the kingdom of Solomon and I will give thee ten sceptres, and two sceptres shall be his for the sake of my servant David and for the sake of Jerusalem the city which I have chosen, . . . that I may place there my name.'*[62] When the twelve tribes of Israel were being divided, Achias the prophet divided his own garment. But because Christ's people cannot be divided, His coat, woven compactly as it was throughout, is not divided by those who acquire it; indivisible, woven all of a piece, compact, it shows that we, who have put on Christ, form a people knit together in harmony. By the sacred symbolism[63] of His garment was proclaimed[64] the oneness of the Church.

8. Can anyone then be so criminal and faithless, so mad in his passion for quarrelling, as to believe it possible that the oneness of God, the garment of the Lord, the Church of Christ should be divided, or dare to divide it himself? Christ admonishes and teaches us in His Gospel: '*And they shall be one flock and one shepherd.*'[65] And does anyone think that in any one place there can be more than one shepherd or more than one flock?[66] The Apostle Paul too commends this same oneness when he begs and exhorts us: *I beseech you brethren by the name of Our Lord Jesus Christ, that you all speak the same thing and that there be no schisms among you; but that you be knit together, having the same mind and the same judgment.*[67] And again he says: *Supporting one another with love, striving to keep the unity of the Spirit in the bond of peace.*[68] Do you think a man can hold his own or survive,[69] when he leaves the Church and sets up a new place and a

separate home for himself? Whereas it was said to
Rahab,[70] in whom the Church was prefigured: *Gather to
thyself in thy house thy father and thy mother and thy brethren
and all thy father's household, and whosoever shall pass outside
through the door of thy house, his blood shall be on his own
head.*[71] So too the sacred meaning of the Pasch[72] lies
essentially in the fact, laid down in Exodus, that the lamb
—slain as a type of Christ—should be eaten in one single
home. God says the words: '*In one house shall it be eaten,
ye shall not cast its flesh outside the house.*'[73] The flesh of
Christ and the Lord's sacred body cannot be cast outside,
nor have believers any other home but the one Church.
This home, this dwelling of concord is indicated and foretold by the Holy Spirit when He says in the Psalms:
*God who maketh those who are of one mind to dwell in a
house.*[74] In God's house, in the Church of Christ do
those of one mind dwell, there they abide in concord
and simplicity.

9. That is also the reason why the Holy Spirit comes in
the form of a dove:[75] it is a simple joyous creature, not
bitter with gall, not biting savagely, without vicious
tearing claws; it loves[76] to dwell with humankind, it keeps
to one house for assembling; when they mate they hatch[77]
their young together, when they fly anywhere they keep
their formation, the resorts they live in are shared in
common, by their billing too they pay tribute to concord
and peace, in all things they fulfil the law of unanimity.
The same is the simplicity of the Church which we need
to learn, this is the charity we must acquire, that we may
imitate the doves in our love for the brethren,[78] and rival
lambs and sheep in their meekness and gentleness. How
can a Christian breast harbour[79] the fierceness of wolves
and the madness of dogs and the deadly venom of snakes

and the blood-lust of wild beasts? It is a blessing when such men break away from the Church:[80] it prevents their preying upon the doves and sheep of Christ with their savage and poisonous influence. It is impossible to join and combine the bitter with the sweet, darkness with the light, rain with fair weather, war with peace; nor with fertility, sterility; with springs of water, aridity; with calm, the storm.

Let no one think that good men can leave the Church; it is not the grain that the wind carries away, nor the solidly rooted tree that the storm blows down: it is the empty chaff that is swept away by the storm, the weakling trees that are overturned by the blast of the whirlwind. On these men fall the curse and the rod[81] of John the Apostle when he says: *They went out from us, but they were not of us. For if they had been of us, they would have stayed with us.*[82]

Discord and ambition lead to schism. Beware of false prophets (10–11).

10. Heresies have often arisen and still arise because of this, that disgruntled minds will quarrel, or disloyal trouble-makers[83] will not keep the unity. But these things the Lord allows and endures, leaving man's freedom unimpaired,[84] so that when our minds and hearts are tested by the touchstone of truth, the unswerving faith of those who are approved may appear in the clearest light. This is foretold by the Holy Spirit through the Apostle when he says: *There must be also heresies, that those approved may be manifest among you.*[85] Thus are the faithful proved, thus the faithless discovered; thus too even before the day of judgment, already here below, the souls of the just and unjust are distinguished, and the wheat is separated from

the chaff.[86] This explains why certain people,[86a] backed
by their hot-headed associates, seize authority for themselves without any divine sanction, making themselves
into prelates regardless of the rules of appointment,[87]
and, having no one to confer the episcopate upon them,
assume the title of Bishop on their own authority.[87a]
In the Psalms the Holy Spirit describes these men as
sitting in the chair of pestilence;[88] they are pests and
plagues to the faith, snake-tongued deceivers, skilled
corruptors of the truth, spewing deadly venom from their
poisonous fangs; whose speech spreads like a canker;[89]
whose preaching[90] injects a fatal virus in the hearts and
breasts of all.

11. Against such men as these the Lord cries out, from
these He curbs and recalls His erring people, saying:
*'Hearken not to the talk of the false prophets, for the visions of
their heart deceive them. They speak, but not out of the mouth
of the Lord. They say to those who reject the word of the Lord:
"You shall have peace"; and to all who walk according to their
own desires, and to him who walks in the error of his heart: "No
evil shall befall thee."'*[91] *'I did not speak to them, and they
prophesied of themselves. Had they taken their stand on my
support and listened to my words, had they taught them to my
people, I should have converted them from their evil thoughts.'*[92]
It is these same men whom the Lord indicates and censures
when He says: *'They have forsaken me, the fountain of the
water of life, and they have digged out for themselves crumbling
cisterns, which cannot hold the water.'*[93] Whereas there can
be but the one baptism,[94] they think they can baptize;
they have abandoned the fountain of life, yet promise the
life and grace of the waters of salvation. It is not cleansing
that men find there, but soiling; their sins are not washed
away but only[95] added to. That 'new birth' does not bring

forth sons unto God, but to the devil. Born of a lie, they cannot inherit what the truth has promised; begotten by the faithless, they are deprived of the grace of faith. The reward for those 'in peace'[96] can never come to men who have broken the peace of the Lord by the frenzy of dissent.

'Two or three gathered in my name': unity recommended, not sectarianism (12–13).

12. Nor let certain people[97] deceive themselves by a foolish interpretation of Our Lord's words: '*Wherever two or three are gathered together in my name, I am with them.*'[98] Corruptors and false interpreters of the Gospel, they quote the end and ignore what has gone before, repeating part of it and dishonestly suppressing the rest; just as they have cut themselves off from the Church, so they cut up the sense of a single passage. For Our Lord was urging His disciples to unanimity and peace when He said: '*I say to you that if two of you agree on earth concerning anything whatsoever you shall ask, it shall be done for you by my Father who is in heaven. For wherever two or three are gathered together in my name, I am with them.*'[99]—showing that it was not the number but the unanimity of those praying that counted most. '*If two of you,*' He said, '*agree on earth*': He put unanimity first, He gave the precedence to peace and concord; we must agree together loyally and sincerely[100] —that was what He taught. But what sort of agreement will a man make with another if he is out of agreement with the body of the Church itself and with the brethren as a whole? How can two or three gather together in Christ's name, if they have obviously cut themselves off from Christ and His Gospel? For it is not we who have left them, but they who have left us,[101] and by setting up

conventicles in opposition[102] and thus creating new sects
and schisms, they have cut themselves off from the source
and origin of [the Christian] realities.[103]

No, Our Lord is speaking of His Church; He is telling
those[104] who are in the Church, that if they are of one
mind, if, as He commanded and bade, even two or three
gather and pray in unison, they shall,[104a] though but two
or three, obtain from God's majesty what they ask for.
'*Wherever two or three shall be,*' He says, '*I am with them,*'
that is, with those who are without guile and peaceable,
with those who fear God and obey His commands. He
said that He would be with a mere 'two or three,' just as
once He was with the three youths in the fiery furnace,
and because they were guileless before God and persevered
in harmony with one another, He refreshed them with a
dew-laden breeze in the midst of the encircling flames.[105]
So too was He with His two imprisoned Apostles[106]
because they were guileless and in harmony; He Himself
opened the bars of their prison and set His faithful preachers
in the market place once more, to announce the word to
the crowds. Therefore when He lays down in His commands: '*Wherever two or three shall be, I am with them,*' He
does not mean to take men away from the Church which
He founded and built Himself, but He condemns the discord of the faithless; and with His own lips He commends
concord to His faithful, by making clear that He is with
two or three who pray in harmony, rather than with any
number of dissenters, and that more can be obtained by
the united prayers of a few than by the petitioning of many
who are in disagreement.

13. For the same reason, when He was legislating for
prayer, He added: '*And when you shall stand for prayer,
forgive if you have aught against any man, that your Father*

also who is in heaven may forgive you your sins.'[107] And so, if a man comes to the sacrifice with strife in his heart, He calls him back from the altar and bids him be reconciled to his brother first, and then in peace of soul return and make his offering to God.[108] For neither did God have respect to the gifts of Cain:[109] such a man could not have God at peace with him when he was torn with jealousy towards his brother and at war with him. What sort of peace then do the enemies of the brethren promise themselves? What sort of sacrifice do they think they offer as opponents of the priests?[110] Do they think that Christ is with them in their gatherings, when those gatherings are outside the Church of Christ?

To leave the Church, a breach of charity—thereafter even martyrdom unavailing for salvation (14–15).

14. Nay, though they should suffer death for the confession of the Name, the guilt of such men is not removed[111] even by their blood; the grievous irremissible sin[112] of schism is not purged even by martyrdom. No martyr can he be who is not in the Church: the kingdom shall be closed to him who has deserted her who is destined to be its queen.[113] Peace is what Christ gave us; He bade us be united in heart and mind: He enjoined on us to keep intact and unimpaired the pledges of our love and charity; no one can claim the martyr's name who has broken off his love for the brethren. This is the Apostle Paul's teaching and witness: *And if I should have faith so that I could remove mountains and have not charity, I am nothing. And if I should distribute all my goods in food, and if I should deliver my body to be burned and have not charity, I profit nothing. Charity is great-hearted, charity is kind, charity envieth not, is not puffed up, is not provoked to anger,*

dealeth not perversely, thinketh no evil, loveth all things,
believeth all things, hopeth all things, beareth all things.
Charity shall never fall away.[114]

'Never,' he says, 'shall charity fall away.' It will persist
in the kingdom for ever, it will continue for all eternity
in the close union of the brethren together. Disunion
cannot lead to the kingdom of heaven; and Christ, who
said: '*This is my commandment, that ye love one another, as I*
have loved you,'[115] cannot reward him[116] who has violated
the love of Christ by disloyal dissension. He who has not
charity, has not God. Hear the voice of the blessed Apostle
John: *God,* he says, *is love; and he that abideth in God*
abideth in love, and God abideth in him.[117] Those who have
refused to be of one mind in the Church of God cannot
therefore be abiding with God. Though they be cast in
the fire and burnt in the flames, though they be exposed
to the wild beasts and lay down their lives, this will not
win them the crown of faith, but will be the penalty for
their unfaithfulness; not the glorious consummation of
holy valour, but an end put to recklessness.[118] Such a man
may be put to death; crowned he cannot be. If he calls
himself a Christian, the devil too often calls himself the
Christ, and is a liar; Our Lord Himself foretelling it:
'*Many will come in my name, saying, "I am Christ,"* and
will deceive many.'[119] Just as the devil is not Christ though
he tricks people by the name, so a man cannot be taken
for[120] a Christian who does not abide in Christ's Gospel
and in the true faith.[121]

15. No doubt, prophesying and casting out devils and
working great miracles on earth are sublime and wonderful
achievements, and yet not everyone who does them comes
to the kingdom of heaven, unless he keeps carefully to
the straight path of justice. So does Our Lord announce it:

'*Many will say to me in that day:* "*Lord, Lord, have we not prophesied in Thy name and turned out devils in Thy name and done great miracles in Thy name?*" *And then I will say to them:* "*I never knew you. Begone from me, you that work iniquity!*" '[122] Justice of life[123] is needed if one is to conciliate God[124] who is our Judge; His commands and warnings must be obeyed if our merits are to receive their reward. Our Lord in the Gospel, when giving us in summary the direction for our hope and faith, said: ' " *The Lord thy God is one Lord, and thou shalt love the Lord thy God with thy whole heart and with thy whole soul and with thy whole strength.*" *This comes first, and the second is like to it:* "*Thou shalt love thy neighbour as thyself.*"[125] *On these two commandments dependeth the whole law and the prophets.*'[126] Unity and love together He taught with the weight of His authority; He embraced all the prophets and the law in the two commandments. But what unity is maintained, what love practised or even imagined by one who, mad with the frenzy of discord, splits the Church, destroys the faith, disturbs the peace, casts charity to the winds, desecrates the Sacrament?[127]

Revolts against the priests of God: His judgments in the Old Testament. Such rebels worse than the lapsed (16–19).

16. This evil, my faithful brethren, first showed itself long since, but now the disastrous malignity of the same evil has increased, and the poisonous bane of obstinate heresies and schisms is growing and multiplying, for so it was to be in the decline of the world, as the Holy Spirit foretold and warned us through the Apostle: *In the last days,* he says, *shall there be troublous times. Men shall be self-centred, proud, haughty, covetous, blasphemers; heedless of their*

parents' word, ungrateful, wicked, without affection, covenant-breakers, informers, incontinent, unmerciful, no lovers of good, traitors, insolent, puffed up with conceit, lovers of pleasures more than of God, presenting a façade of religion, but denying the power thereof. . . . Of this sort are those who creep into houses and ravish silly women laden with sins, who are led away with divers desires, ever learning and never attaining to the knowledge of the truth. And as Jannes and Mambres resisted Moses, so these also resist the truth, . . . but they shall not proceed any further. For their ineptitude shall be manifest to all men, as theirs also was.[128] Whatever was foretold is being realized, and as the end of the world approaches, men and times alike are being tested by it. As the Enemy rages more and more, error misleads, conceit puffs up, jealousy inflames, covetousness blinds, wickedness depraves, pride inflates, discord exacerbates, anger begets recklessness.[129]

17. We must not, however, be troubled or dismayed by the gross and sudden faithlessness of many; rather should it strengthen our own faith because of the fulfilment of its prediction. As some people have begun to turn out like this because it was foretold, so must the rest of the brethren take heed against them,[130] because this too was predicted when Our Lord instructed us: '*But do ye take heed: behold I have foretold you all things.*'[131] I implore you to avoid men of that stamp, and to protect your persons, nay your very ears, from their baleful conversation as from some deadly plague, according to the Scripture: *Hedge in thy ears with thorns, and hear not a wicked tongue;*[132] and again: *Wicked conversations corrupt good characters.*[133] Our Lord's teaching warns us to withdraw from such men: '*They are blind leaders of the blind,*' He says. '*The blind man leading the blind, they will both fall into the pit.*'[134] Whoever is separated from the Church must be avoided and fled

from; such a man is wrong-headed, he is a sinner and self-condemned.[135] Does a man think he is with Christ when he acts in opposition to the bishops of Christ, when he cuts himself off from the society of His clergy and people? He is bearing arms against the Church, he is waging war upon God's institutions. An enemy of the altar, a rebel against the sacrifice of Christ; giving up faith for perfidy,[136] religion for sacrilege; an unruly servant, an undutiful son and hostile brother, despising the bishops and deserting the priests of God, he presumes to set up a new altar,[137] to raise unauthorized voices in a rival liturgy,[138] to profane the reality of the divine Victim[139] by pseudo-sacrifices, forgetting that whoever opposes God's institution[140] is punished for his reckless insolence[141] by divine retribution.

18. Thus it was that Core, Dathan, and Abiron, who wanted to establish their claim to sacrifice in opposition to Moses and to Aaron the priest, immediately paid the penalty for their attempt. The solid earth split and yawned in a deep abyss; as the ground parted, the gap swallowed them alive where they stood.[142] Not only were the principal agents struck by the fury of God's anger, but their two hundred and fifty associates and followers who had joined them in the same wild outrage, were summarily punished: they were consumed by the fire that was evoked by the Lord.[143] This was to warn[144] us and show that any attempt made by the wicked deliberately to frustrate the appointment[145] of God, is done against God Himself.[146] Thus it was, too, that when king Ozias, taking up the thurible, insisted on offering sacrifice contrary to God's law, and refused to desist or obey Azarias the priest when he tried to restrain him, the wrath of God put him to confusion by striking him with the stain of leprosy on his

forehead[147]—that part of his body being marked for
offending the Lord where those who win the Lord's
favour[148] are sealed.[149] And the children of Aaron who
placed *strange fire* on the altar, such as the Lord had not
commanded, were immediately destroyed in the sight of
the Lord by His vengeance.[150]

19. Now[151] these are imitated and followed closely by
those men who, disregarding God's teaching,[152] crave for
strange doctrines and introduce authorities of human
origin; Our Lord rebukes and castigates them in His
Gospel: '*You reject the commandment of God that you may
establish your own tradition.*'[153] This crime is a greater one
than that which the lapsed, no doubt, have committed;[154]
but these, becoming penitents for their crime, are at least
calling upon God's mercy by making satisfaction for it to
the full.[155] In their case the Church is being sought and
appealed to, in the other the Church is repudiated; in the
first there may have been a yielding to pressure, in the
second the will persists in its guilt;[156] in the first the man
who fell hurt only himself, in the second the instigator of
heresy and schism has deceived many by dragging them
after him; in the first case harm is done to a single soul,
in the second many are imperilled. Manifestly, the former
recognizes that he has sinned,[157] and he grieves and sorrows
for it, but the latter is not only puffed up with his sin and
self-satisfied in his crimes, but he separates the sons from
their Mother, entices the sheep from their shepherd, upsets
the holy ordinances of God.[158] And whereas the lapsed
has only sinned once, the other continues to sin each day.
Lastly, the lapsed can by subsequent martyrdom obtain
the promises of the kingdom;[159] but the other, if he be out
of the Church when put to death, cannot come to the
rewards which are prepared for the Church.[160]

Bad example of a few 'confessors.' Their confession no guarantee.
Disowned by their fellows (20–22).

20. Nor should anyone be surprised, dearest brethren, that even from among the confessors certain men should stoop to this, and then that some of them should also commit such grievous, such unspeakable sins.[161] For confession does not make a man immune from the snares of the devil, nor, living in the world as he still does, is he thereby guaranteed permanent security against its temptations and dangers, or against its surprise attacks; otherwise[162] we should never see in confessors the dishonesties, and the rapes, and the adulteries which we now witness to our sorrow and distress in some of them. Whoever the confessor may be, he is not greater nor better than Solomon, nor dearer to God than he; and yet Solomon only retained the favour which the Lord had granted him so long as he walked in the ways of the Lord, but when he departed from the way of the Lord, he also lost the favour of the Lord. That is why it is written: '*Hold fast that which thou hast, lest another take thy crown.*'[163] For the Lord would never[164] have threatened that the crown would be taken,[165] unless the loss of justice necessarily means that its crown is lost too.

21. Confession is a first step towards glory, not the final crown of merit; it is not the ultimate achievement[166] but a beginning of greatness, and since it is written: '*He that shall persevere unto the end, he shall be saved,*'[167] whatever comes before the end is only a step in the climb to the heights of salvation, not the goal, which is the conquest of the peak's summit.

He is a confessor, no doubt;[168] but after his confession he is in all the greater danger, because the Adversary has been the more provoked.

He is a confessor: that only calls for the greater loyalty to Our Lord's Gospel, since it was by means of the Gospel that he came to deserve such an honour from Our Lord.[169] *'To whom much is given, much is required of him; and on whom the more dignity is bestowed, of him the more service is demanded.'*[170] Let none be lost through the example of a confessor; let none learn to be unjust, or arrogant, or unfaithful because of a confessor's behaviour.

He is a confessor: let him be humble and peaceful, let his actions show modesty and self-control, so that, as he is named a confessor of Christ, he may imitate the Christ whom he confesses. For if Christ said: *'He that extolleth himself shall be humbled, and he that humbleth himself shall be exalted,'*[171] and if He Himself, the Word and the power and the wisdom of God His Father,[172] was exalted by the Father because He humbled Himself on earth, how can ostentation appeal to Him who not only enjoined on us humility in His law, but was Himself rewarded for His humility by His Father with the most glorious of all names?[173]

He is a confessor of Christ; yes, provided that[174] he does not later cause the majesty and good name of Christ to be blasphemed.[175] Let not the tongue which has confessed Christ be spiteful or mischievous; let it not be clamorous with altercations and quarrels; after its glorious confession let it not hiss with serpent's venom against the brethren and the priests of God. If nevertheless[176] he does afterwards become guilty and odious, if he fritters away his reputation as a confessor by the evil of his ways, if he stains his life with filth and infamy, and if, in consequence, he leaves the Church to which he owes his becoming a confessor, if he breaks up its harmony and unity, and so in place of loyalty to his first faith adopts unfaithfulness,[177] he cannot flatter himself that his confession has predestined him to the reward of glory; on the contrary, it will only increase the retribution that awaits him.[178]

22. For example, Judas was himself one of the Apostles chosen by Our Lord, and yet afterwards Judas betrayed his Lord. But the faith and loyalty of the Apostles was not destroyed because Judas the traitor left their company. So too now, the holiness and good name of the confessors is not straightway impaired because some of their number have broken faith. The blessed Apostle says in one of his epistles: *For what if some of them have fallen away from the faith? Has their unfaithfulness made the faith of God without effect? God forbid! For God is true, but every man a liar.*[179] The majority of the confessors, and the better ones, stand strong in their faith and true to Our Lord's law and discipline,[180] and, remembering that it was in the Church that by God's goodness the grace was given them, they are not such as to break from the Church's unity.[181] Indeed their faith has acquired the greater lustre by this, that, refusing to join in the unfaithfulness of those who had been united to them[182] by their confession together, they have kept free from all infection of that crime; shining with the bright truth of the Gospel, radiant with Our Lord's own pure and spotless light, the praise which they deserve for maintaining the unity of Christ is as great as the victory which they won in their engagement with the devil.

Ignore the mischief-makers; return to unity, in the peace of Christ (23–24).

23. For my part I hope, dearest brethren, and I urge and press it upon you, that, if possible, not one of the brethren should perish, but that our Mother[183] should have the happiness of clasping to her bosom all our people in one

like-minded body. But if some of the leaders of schism
who are responsible for our divisions persist in their blind
and obstinate folly, if advice for their own good fails to
bring them back to the way of salvation, let the rest of
you—whether you followed them in sheer simplicity and
under misapprehension, or were led astray by their deceit-
ful cunning—break away from their ensnaring falsehood,
set yourselves free from the errors into which you have
strayed, find once more the straight path of the way to
heaven.[184] Hear the Apostle's message: *We bid you in the
name of Our Lord Jesus Christ to withdraw from all the
brethren who walk disorderly and not according to the tradition
which they have received from us.*[185] And again he says: *Let
no man deceive you with vain words, for because of that cometh
the anger of God upon the children of insolence. Be ye not
therefore partakers with them.*[186] One must withdraw from
those engaged in sin—rather,[187] one must fly from them,
lest by joining in their evil course and so taking the wrong
road of crime, one should, on leaving the true way,[188]
become involved in the same guilt oneself. God is one,
and Christ is one, and His Church is one; one is the faith,
and one the people cemented together by harmony[188a]
into the strong unity of a body. That unity cannot be
split; that one body cannot be divided by any cleavage of
its structure, nor cut up in fragments with its vitals torn
apart. Nothing that is separated from the parent stock can
ever live or breathe apart; all hope of its salvation[189] is lost.

24. We are admonished by the Holy Spirit: *Who is the
man that desireth life, and loveth to see most blessed days?
Restrain thy tongue from evil and thy lips from speaking
deceitfully. Turn away from evil and do good, seek after peace
and pursue it.*[190] A son of peace must seek after peace and
pursue it; whoever knows and loves the bond of charity,

must restrain his tongue from the evil of dissension. Among the divine commands and instructions for salvation which Our Lord gave on the very eve of His passion, He included this: '*Peace I commit to you, my peace I give you.*'[191] This is the inheritance which He has left us: with the maintenance of peace, He was assuring us of all the gifts and rewards which He had promised. If we are the heirs of Christ, let us abide in the peace of Christ; if we are the sons of God, we must be lovers of peace. '*Blessea are the peacemakers,*' He said, '*for they shall be called the sons of God.*'[192] Sons of God must be makers of peace, gentle of heart, guileless of tongue, harmonious of sentiment, sincerely attached to one another by the bond of a common mind.[193]

Imitate the generosity of the apostolic Church; such care for unity a safeguard from the devil (25–27).

25. This common mind prevailed once, in the time of the Apostles;[194] this was the spirit in which the new community of the believers obeyed Our Lord's commands and maintained charity with one another. The Scriptures are witness to it: *But the crowd of those who had come to believe acted with one mind and soul.*[195] And again: *They were all persevering with one mind in prayer with the women and Mary who had been the mother of Jesus, and with His brethren.*[196] And that was the reason why their prayers were efficacious, that was why they could be confident of obtaining whatever they asked of God's mercy.

26. But amongst us, that unity of mind has weakened in proportion as the generosity of our charity[197] has crumbled away. In those days, they would sell their houses and estates and lay up to themselves treasure in heaven[198] by giving the money to the Apostles for distribution to

those in need. But now, we do not even give tithes on our patrimony, and whereas Our Lord tells us to sell, we buy instead and accumulate. To such an extent has active faith withered among us, to such an extent have our people lost their old steadfastness in belief. That is why Our Lord says in His Gospel, with an eye on our times: '*The Son of man, when He cometh, shall He find, think you, faith on earth?*'[199] We see what He foretold happening before our eyes. As to fear of God, or sense of justice,[200] or charity, or good works[201]—faith inspires us to none of them. No one thinks of the fears that the future holds in store: the day of the Lord and the wrath of God, the punishments that await unbelievers, the eternal torments appointed for the betrayers of their faith—no one gives them a thought. Whatever a believing conscience should fear, our conscience, because it no longer believes, fears not at all. If only it believed, it would take heed; if it took heed, it would escape.

27. Let us do our utmost, dearest brethren, to rouse ourselves, and breaking off the sleep of our past inertia, give our minds to the observance and fulfilment of Our Lord's commands. Let us be such as He told us to be: '*Let your loins be girt and your lamps burning, and you yourselves like to men who wait for their lord when he shall come from the wedding; that when he cometh and knocketh they may open to him. Blessed are those servants whom the Lord when He cometh shall find watching.*'[202] Our loins must be girt, lest when the day comes for the campaign, it find us encumbered with trappings. Let our light shine brightly in good works, so that it may lead us from the darkness of this world into the spendour of eternal light. Let us await the sudden coming of Our Lord, ever attentive and on the alert, so that when He shall knock, our faith may be watching,

ready to receive from Our Lord the reward of its vigil.
Were but these commands obeyed, were but these
warnings and precepts observed—it is impossible that we
should be tricked and overcome[203] by the devil in our
sleep; from being watchful servants we shall, under
Christ's lordship, come to reign ourselves.

NOTES

LIST OF ABBREVIATIONS

ACW	Ancient Christian Writers (Westminster, Md.—London 1946–)
A, M, R, S, V, W	Some of the older MSS of Cyprian
e, f, k	Some of the (fragmentary) MSS of the Old Latin New Testament
Blaise-Chirat	*Dictionnaire latin-français des auteurs chrétiens* (Strasbourg 1954)
de Ghellinck	J. de Ghellinck, etc., *Pour l'histoire du mot 'Sacramentum.'* I. *Les Anténicéens* (Spicilegium sacrum Lovaniense 3, Louvain 1924)
Grasmüller	O. Grasmüller, *Koordinierende, subordinierende und fragende Partikeln bei St. Cyprian von Karthago* (Erlangen 1933)
JTS	*Journal of Theological Studies* (Oxford 1899– [New Series 1950–])
LCP (5, 6, 8, 9)	Latinitas christiana primaeva. Studia ad sermonem latinum pertinentia (Nijmegen):

      5. J. Schrijnen—C. Mohrmann, *Studien zur Syntax der Briefe des hl. Cyprian*, I (1936)

      6. The same, II (1937)

      8. H. Janssen, *Kultur und Sprache. Zur Geschichte der alten Kirche im Spiegel der Sprachentwicklung: von Tertullian bis Cyprian* (1938)

      9. P. A. H. J. Merkx, *Zur Syntax der Kasus und Tempora in den Traktaten des hl. Cyprian* (1939)

LXX	The Septuagint: the chief Greek version of the Old Testament
Martin	*S. Cypriani De lapsis*, ed. Jos. Martin (Florilegium Patristicum 21, Bonn 1930)
Matzkow	*Itala. Das Neue Testament in altlateinischer Überlieferung* (A. Jülicher—W. Matzkow) I: *Matthäus-Evangelium* (Berlin 1938); II: *Marcus-Evangelium* (Berlin 1940)

O. L.	The Old Latin Versions of the Scriptures, subsequently replaced by the Vulgate
PG	J. P. Migne, Patrologia graeca (Paris 1857–66)
PL	J. P. Migne, Patrologia latina (Paris 1844–55)
RAC	Reallexikon für Antike und Christentum (Stuttgart 1950–)
RE	A. Pauly, G. Wissowa, W. Kroll, etc., Real-Encyclopädie der classischen Altertumswissenschaft (Stuttgart 1893–)
Rönsch	H. Rönsch, *Itala und Vulgata* (2 ed. Marburg 1875)
SCA	The Catholic University of America Studies in Christian Antiquity (Washington 1941–)
von Soden	H. von Soden, *Das lateinische Neue Testament in Afrika zur Zeit Cyprians* (Texte und Untersuchungen 33, Leipzig 1909)
Souter	A. Souter, *A Glossary of Later Latin to 600 A.D.* (Oxford 1949)
TLL	Thesaurus linguae latinae (Berlin, Göttingen, etc. 1900–)
Vulg.	The Vulgate: the Latin version of the Scriptures prepared by St. Jerome
Watson	E. W. Watson, *The Style and Language of St. Cyprian* (Studia biblica et ecclesiastica IV, Oxford 1896) 189–324
ZKT	*Zeitschrift für katholische Theologie* (Innsbruck 1877–)

INTRODUCTION

[1] See St. Cyprian's treatise *De mortalitate*, edited—with a commentary and translation—by M. L. Hannan (Cath. Univ. of America Patristic Studies 36, Washington 1933).

[2] Cf. C. Favez, 'La fuite de saint Cyprien lors de la persécution de Décius,' *Rev. études lat.* 19 (1941) 191–201.

[3] *The Lapsed*. This title, Latin-sounding as it is, has been kept in preference to 'the Fallen' or 'the Backsliders' (!) etc., because those referred to formed a very definite class of 'fallen,' namely those Christians in the Roman Empire who apostatized under threat of torture or death. Besides, the term is current among those interested in early Church History.

[4] The sacrament of Penance, as administered in Cyprian's time, differed in many respects from modern practice. It involved being placed in the ranks of the 'penitents' for a considerable time where prayer, fasting, and repeated acts of humiliation were expected of them. It is not clear whether the penitents, like the catechumens, had to leave the divine service before the Mass of the faithful began; but if they stayed, as is perhaps more likely, they were certainly debarred from receiving Communion. When they had completed their time, they were solemnly admitted back into the body of the faithful and so could receive Communion once more. In this readmission to the fellowship, or reconciliation, the people as a whole had a share, though the essential part of the ceremony was the laying on of hands by the bishop. It was he who determined the length of the penance and controlled its due observance.—Cyprian gives a summary of the ordinary process in *Ep.* 16.2: *cum in minoribus peccatis* (i.e. less serious than idolatry) *agant paenitentiam iusto tempore, et secundum disciplinae ordinem ad exomologesin veniant, et per manus inpositionem episcopi et cleri ius communicationis accipiant*, . . . ; cf. also *Ep.* 17.2 and *De laps.* 16, below, with nn. 66–68.—The fullest study of Cyprian's evidence for Penance, liturgically and dogmatically, is that of K. Rahner: 'Die Busslehre des hl. Cyprian von Karthago,' in ZKT 74 (1952) 257–76 and 381–438. For a short summary of the dogmatic significance of Cyprian's teaching on Penance, cf. B. Poschmann in *Handbuch der Dogmengeschichte* IV.3: 'Busse und letzte Ölung' (Freiburg i. Br. 1951) 31 f., and his fuller treatment of the subject in *Paenitentia secunda* (Theophaneia 1, Bonn 1940) 398–424.

[5] The text of the edict has not come down to us and its exact scope remains uncertain. Some would confine its application to those suspected of being Christians. But it must have included others—perhaps anyone suspected of disloyalty to the empire—in view of the Egyptian papyri. (Cf. J. Zeiller in *History of the Primitive Church* [Lebreton and Zeiller], Eng. trans. vol. 4 [London 1948] 647 ff. ; also A. Alföldi in *Camb. Anc. Hist.* 12 [1939] 202 ff., and H. Lietzmann, *ibid.* 521.)

[6] Quite apart from the fasting etc., the public humiliation of advertising oneself as a sinner formed no small part of the 'penance,' though this did not necessarily involve the publication of the sins committed. In n. 4, above, *exhomologesis* is used in the technical sense of the sinner's part in the ceremony of reconciliation; similarly *Ep.* 18.1. So too *De laps.* 16, where cf. n. 66. (Hartel spells the word *exomologesis*, acc. *-im* or *-in*. The evidence of the MSS seems to favour *exhomologesis*, acc. *-in*.)

[6a] *De ecclesiae catholicae unitate.* The title raises three problems: a) Did Cyprian use the word *catholica*, or should we read, *De ecclesiae unitate*? b) Was he speaking of the universal Church or of the local church? c) Does *unitas* mean uniqueness, 'oneness' (thus denying the possibility of a multiplicity of Churches), or does it mean simply 'unity,' in the sense of cohesion of the parts together?

a) Because some MSS omit *catholicae* in the title, and Cyprian does not use the expression *ecclesia catholica* in the body of the treatise (nor at all before the Novatianist schism), H. Koch adds this to his reasons for dating the treatise before that schism (*Cyprianische Untersuchungen* [Bonn 1926] 102–107). But as C. H. Turner pointed out in his review of Koch's work, the expression *ecclesia catholica* must have been well established and familiar even in the 2nd century (*English Hist. Rev.* 43 [1928] 247), and H. Janssen considers that the balance of evidence of the MSS favours the presence of *catholicae* in the title as against Koch's *a priori* arguments (LCP 8.18 n. 2). But the question of its wording is of little importance in comparison with that of the scope of the treatise itself.

b) Cf. Introd. 5–8. Some have held that Cyprian was only dealing with the unity of the local church; so, e.g. O. Casel (*Revue bénédictine* 30 [1913] 413–20), and many have followed him. No doubt, the main purpose of the treatise is to secure unity within the local church, for Cyprian was preaching to his own people, who were being torn this way and that. But in doing so, he embraces in his vision the hundreds of local churches which make up the Church as a whole (cf. ch. 5). He argues that because that Church was founded on Peter, it is *unique*;

and because it is unique, *unity* must exist both between the local churches and within each one of them. This latter unity is secured by the uniqueness of the spiritual authority exercised there, vested as it is in one man, who has derived it ultimately from the authority uniquely conferred on Peter; for when he was made a bishop, he received it from men who had themselves already inherited it from Peter. Once a bishop has been duly consecrated to a see and has not broken away from the 'concord of bishops' of the universal Church, anyone else claiming authority in that church is an intruder, a schismatic. In this way the 'uniqueness' of the Church of Christ demands the 'unity' of the local church.

c) The word *unitas* does duty for both these related ideas, and one might translate it either by 'Oneness,' which underlines uniqueness, or by 'Unity,' which primarily signifies coherence and denies division. Furthermore, with their different emphases, each of these words includes both ideas. However, Cyprian was directly fighting *schism*, and if he appealed to the uniqueness of the Church, it was only to defend it against disunity. Therefore the purpose of the treatise is perhaps better represented by 'Unity,' which has the advantage of being the traditional title, whereas 'Oneness,' though representing the more basic idea contained in *unitas*, would be a novelty, with a certain strangeness clinging to the word. As for the presence or absence of the word *catholicae* in the title, it cannot affect the scope of the treatise, which undoubtedly deduces its teaching on the local church from the nature of the universal, catholic Church.

[7] Cf. J. Chapman, 'Les interpolations dans le traité de S. Cyprien sur l'Unité de l'Eglise,' in *Revue bénédictine* 19 (1902) 246–54; 357–73. Harnack (*Theologische Literaturzeitung* [1903] 262 f.) approved, and Hugo Koch used this view in his polemical works, thus excluding Rome from the scope of the *De unitate*.

[8] Cf. M. Bévenot, *St. Cyprian's 'De Unitate' chap. 4 in the Light of the Manuscripts* (Analecta Gregoriana 11, Rome 1937) 66–77.

[9] Cf. *Ep.* 44 ff.

[10] *Ep.* 54.4; cf. *Ep.* 46, 47, 49, 51, 52, 53, and 54.

[11] 'The generally received text' is universally recognized as genuine, but its precise meaning is open to discussion even among Catholics. As for the other text, not only is its meaning disputed, but its significance for estimating Cyprian's outlook will be variously estimated according as it is regarded 1) either as a later forgery: so H. Koch *passim*, and J. Le Moyne, 'Saint Cyprien est-il bien l'auteur de la rédaction brève du "De Unitate" chapitre 4 ?' in *Rev. bénéd.* 63 (1953) 70–115, or as

coming from Cyprian's own hand; and again, on the latter supposition,
2) either as a revision made by Cyprian himself (Chapman, Harnack,
d'Alès, E. Caspar, K. Adam), or as his original text which he later
modified to the 'generally received text' (Batiffol, T. A. Lacey, D. van
den Eynde, O. Perler, Abbot B. C. Butler). Palaeographical and other
reasons for this latter view will be found in the study referred to above
in n. 8; a full discussion of all the evidence would be out of place here,
but some indications will be found below in the notes to that treatise.
Cf. also M. Bévenot, '"Primatus Petro datur," St. Cyprian on the
Papacy,' in JTS n.s. 5 (1954) 19–35, where Dom Le Moyne's criticisms
are answered.

[12] Most significant perhaps is *Ep.* 59.9, on which cf. M. Bévenot,
'"A Bishop is responsible to God alone": St. Cyprian,' in *Mélanges
Lebreton=Rech. de science relig.* 39 (1951) 399–415.

[13] His theory was one thing, the living tradition of the Church in
which he immersed himself from the moment of his conversion was
another. If he ever came to see the insufficiency of his theory and
completed it by a better appreciation of Rome's real position in the
Church, it will have been through the memory of his relations with
Rome in the past, and of what his life as a Christian and as a bishop
had so often prompted him to do. Cf. the article mentioned at
the end of n. 11 above; also Bévenot, 'St. Cyprian and the
Papacy: Musings on an old Problem,' *Dublin Rev.* 228 (1954) 161–68;
307–315.

[14] 'Communio und Primat,' in *Miscellanea hist. pont.* 7 (Rome 1943)
40 f.

[15] The text of the Bible in the Latin versions which existed before
St. Jerome's 'Vulgate' is still an open field of research. The African
Church seems to have had a fairly uniform text (Tertullian, Cyprian,
Augustine). Cyprian's quotations from the Old Testament have been
commented on in the notes, some indication being given of their
dependence on the Greek (LXX). Variations from the Vulgate New
Testament have also been noticed. (For Epistles and Apocalypse, cf.
Novum Testamentum latine secundum editionem S. Hieronymi [Oxford],
begun in 1889 by J. Wordsworth and H. J. White, and, with a
succession of collaborators, brought to a successful conclusion by
Prof. H. F. D. Sparks in 1954. Practically all the known evidence
of the O.L. readings is there collated, mostly from the early
Latin Fathers. Some are also given for Acts.) Though no attempt at
completeness has been made here, sufficient has perhaps been given
to indicate the complexity of the problems involved. The situation will improve with the progress of the work of the monks

of Beuron, who are engaged on the publication of the *Vetus Latina.*

[16] E. W. Watson, *The Style and Language of Cyprian*, in Studia Biblica et Ecclesiastica 4 (Oxford 1896) 201. Cf. also E. Norden, *Die antike Kunstprosa* 2 (Leipzig—Berlin 1918) 618–21.

THE LAPSED

1 'our liberty': *securitas nostra*; lit. freedom from care, anxiety, etc.

2 'avenging intervention of God.' The reference is uncertain. Martin (*ad loc.*) implies that Decius's death in the war against the Goths is referred to, and this would seem at first to be the natural explanation. However, Decius was killed in the first days of June, 251 (see RE 15 [1931] *s.v.* 'Messius [9],' 1252 f.), whereas Cyprian returned to his people and delivered this address soon after Easter, which fell on March 23rd that year.

3 'the Enemy,' i.e. the devil.

4 'confessors': those who had confessed their faith in Christ when required to sacrifice to the idols (cf. below, n. 17).

5 'yearned': Cyprian had not seen his flock since he went into hiding.

6 'sacred kiss.' The formal '*pax*' at High Mass today is a relic of this genuine demonstration of love which formed part of the early Christian liturgy. Cf. K.-M. Hofmann, *Philema hagion* (Gütersloh 1938) 36, 123.

7 'your unchanging faith in Him': *semel credidisse*. A reference to the profession of faith made by adults at baptism. The perfect, *credidi*, is in early Christian writers often used with a present sense, 'I believe,' as implying 'I *made* my profession of faith at baptism and *so* believe *now*.' This is not infrequent in Cyprian's letters, as reflecting common Christian usage (LCP 6. 16–18). In his treatises it is rare (LCP 9. 93–97). Perhaps this is because, by Cyprian's time, many had been baptized in infancy, and when writing more carefully, he was conscious of its loss of appropriateness. In fact, here, though he keeps the popular expression, he revives its reference to baptism by inserting *semel*. Cf. Acts 4.32 as Cyprian read it: quoted in *De unit.* ch. 25 and n. 195.

8 At Roman sacrifices, a veil was worn to shield the eye from evil influences. There may be a play on the meaning of *caput* in conjunction with the ideas of freedom and slavery, cf. *deminutio capitis*, etc.

9 *diaboli coronam*. The 'corona' is primarily a wreath or garland worn at sacrifices, feasts, etc. On the practice, cf. K. Baus, *Der Kranz in Antike und Christentum* (Theophaneia 2, Bonn 1940) 7–17. Its religious associations led to its adoption by kings, etc. at their deification. It was also a reward for military valour, and thus we have the martyr's 'crown.'

[10] Cf. J. C. Plumpe, *Mater Ecclesia: an Inquiry into the Concept of the Church as Mother in Early Christianity* (SCA 5, Washington 1943); ch. 6: Cyprian.

[11] For their chastity as for their faith.

[12] 'dear brethren,' reading *fratres dilectissimi* with the early editions and the oldest Oxford MSS.

[13] 'those who have stood firm': *stantes*, in contrast to the *lapsi* in time of persecution. 'The very term *stantes* is identical with, if not borrowed from, the gladiatorial name for the victor' (Watson 292).

[14] 'declare himself': *professus ... est. Professio* is a more general word than *confessio*, which is restricted to faith (esp. in Christ). Here and below, ch. 27 and n. 135a, as also in *Ep.* 30.3, *professio* (or *professus*) is used of the declaration made in the *libelli* (cf. Introd. 5–8); in *Ep.* 30.8, however, of the repudiation of misdeeds; and in *Ep.* 81 it is contrasted with *confessio*, not as its opposite, but to bring out that, when on trial for the faith, the Christian has God in him and speaks *with* Him (*con-*): (in qualification of Watson 293). For *confessio* of sacramental confession, cf. below, ch. 29 n. 146 and ch. 16 n. 66.

[15] *Deo reservari*. It is clear that this phrase here has no reference to judgment in the next life (cf. *Ep.* 55.22, of the justice and mercy of God, *punientis ut corrigat, et cum correxerit reservantis*). So too, then, in the same *Ep.* 55.29: *in ipsa* (sc. *ecclesia*) *Domino reservari*; on which see M. Bévenot, 'The Sacrament of Penance and St. Cyprian's *De lapsis*,' *Theol. Stud.* n.s. 6 (1955) 194 (with n. 74).

[16] 'since ... he had no intention of denying his faith': *idcirco ... quia non erat negaturus*. He was *not going to* deny—and that, not only in intention, but in fact. On *confiteretur* for *confessus esset* ('he would ... have confessed'), cf. LCP 9.123.

[17] '*martyrs ... confessors.*' These names 'are used equally often, and quite indifferently' (Watson 290). Subsequent studies have disproved this. If those who survived torture, or even those still waiting in prison, are ever called 'martyrs,' this is in laudatory acknowledgment of their good will, or else is equivalent to 'martyr-designates.' The concept of *martyrium* included actual death for the faith; cf. *De unit.* 14, and *De mort.* 17 (during a plague): 'I was ready to confess Christ; I had committed myself wholeheartedly to the sufferings of execution; and now I am *deprived of my martyrdom* if death forestalls me [by sickness].' Cf. A. d'Alès, *La théologie de S. Cyprien* (Paris 1922) 362; H. Delehaye, 'Martyr et confesseur,' *Analecta Bollandiana* (1921) 31–33; E. L. Hummel, *The Concept of Martyrdom according to St. Cyprian of Carthage* (SCA 9, Washington 1946) 8–11, 14, 20, 29–33, etc.

[18] *sub apostolis*. This use of *sub*, for 'in the time of' (which is found

from the age of Augustus), suggested originally: 'under the might, or rule, of.' It is striking that Christians came to use it of their bishops (cf. *Ep.* 15.1: *sicut in praeteritis semper sub antecessoribus nostris factum est*). That it had lost all idea of 'under the might of' is shown by *Ep.* 73.17: *alia enim fuit sub apostolis Iudaeorum ratio, alia gentilium condicio*, and by Luke 4.27: *sub Elisaeo propheta* (O.L. and *Vulg.*); cf. LCP 5.121 f. *Sub apostolis* occurs also below, chs. 11 (see n. 47) and 35; and in *De unit.* ch. 25 (n. 194; cf. LCP 9.62 f.).

[19] 'and': *aut ... aut*, used several times by Cyprian for *et ... et*; however, *vel ... vel* in this sense would be normal enough (Watson 315). At this stage of early Christian Latin, writers tended to use copulative *aut* in religious contexts, and copulative *vel* in profane contexts—cf. LCP 6.75–78. Cyprian even uses *aut* for *neque* in *Ep.* 55.12; cf. LCP 5.34.

[20] 'bishops ... clergy': *sacerdotibus ... ministeriis* (or *-stris*). *Sacerdos* stands primarily for 'bishop' in Cyprian and in most of the Christian writers in the following centuries. *Ministri* will here include the rest of the clergy. For details cf. Watson 258 n. and 260 n. See also below, ch. 26 with n. 132.

[21] *in operibus misericordiae*, cf. ch. 35 and n. 171.

[22] Cf. Lev. 19.27 (Cyprian, *Test.* 3.84) and below, ch. 30 with n. 150.

[23] For Cyprian's invective against make-up, cf. *De habitu virginum* chs. 14–17, and below, ch. 30.

[24] Cf. *Test.* 3.62; 1 Cor. 6.15; 2 Cor. 6.14. Allowance must be made for Cyprian's rhetorical manner; but the Church's discouragement of mixed marriages remains.

[25] 'one another': *sibi*; the reflexive pronoun being used for reciprocation. Cf. *Ep.* 63.13 (of the wine and the water in the Eucharist): *nisi utrumque sibi misceatur* (cf. Watson 307).

[26] *hortamento* (lit. 'exhortation'). But Cyprian may have written *ornamento* ('giving them something to be proud of'), which is supported by two important Oxford MSS and also by Augustine, *C. Cresc.* 3.36 (in some MSS); cf. A. Souter, JTS (1931) 424. Augustine repeatedly quoted this catalogue of episcopal misdeeds: cf. Martin, *De laps.* p. 14, l. 6 n.

[27] Ps. 88.31–33. 'statutes': *iustificationes*; 'observe': *observaverint*; 'commands': *praecepta*; 'crimes': *facinora*; 'transgressions': *delicta*; 'scourges': *flagellis*. These are characteristic of Cyprian's text as against the Vulg. and most other O.L. texts (cf. *Ep.* 11.2 and 55.22; also Hartel's apparatus on *Test.* 2.1 and 3.57—with *De unit.* 24 and n. 190).

[28] *Christi sacramentum*, i.e. the profession of faith made at baptism.

Here the word *sacramentum* reflects its classical sense of the military oath of allegiance. This is borne out by *minantis inimici* and *prostratus inpetu* in the preceding sentence, as also by *solveretur* here (for the 'breaking' of the oath); *Ep.* 74.8: *divinae militiae sacramenta solvantur.* See J. B. Poukens in *Pour l'histoire du mot 'sacramentum'* (ed. J. de Ghellinck, Louvain 1924) 163; and below, ch. 13 and n. 51.

29 'oppressed': *pressuras*, rendering the Scriptural θλίψις (Watson 289).

30 Deut. 6.13 (to which the quotation is explicitly referred in *Test.* 3.10).—'shalt thou adore': *adorabis*—so most of the Latin authors quote the passage, perhaps influenced by Matt, 4.10. Tertullian alone follows the ordinary LXX reading: *Dominum Deum tuum timebis.* But Codex Alexandrinus reads προσκυνήσεις; which leaves open the nice question whether the O.L. was following a better Greek tradition, or whether both the O.L. and the Cod. Alex. were here influenced by the N.T. Vulg.: *timebis*: 'thou shalt fear the Lord thy God' (Douay). —'and Him only': *illi soli*; so all the Latins, including Tertullian and Vulg., and also Cod. Alex.; otherwise not in the LXX nor the Hebrew.

31 Isa. 2.8 f., following LXX. The chief divergence from the Heb. is represented by 'And I shall not weaken towards them': *et non laxabo illis*; Vulg. *ne ergo dimittas eis*: 'therefore forgive them not' (Douay).

32 Exod. 22.20. 'He that sacrificeth': *sacrificans*; Vulg. *qui immolat*.— 'shall be uprooted': *eradicabitur*; Vulg. *occidetur*: 'shall be put to death' (Douay).

33 Cf. Matt. 10.32 f.

34 'going up [to offer sacrifice]': *ascenderent*, cf. below, n. 36, and ch. 24 n. 114, *Capitolium . . . ascendit*, in the same sense. The Capitol— *Mons Capitolinus*—Rome's ancient citadel and sanctuary of the national gods, had its counterpart or reproduction in many cities in Italy and the provinces, e.g. Capua, Verona, Seville, Treves, Byzantium, Jerusalem, etc. So Carthage too had its own Capitol, and in the atmosphere of persecution 'to go up' to it was a way of saying 'to sacrifice to the gods'; and *Capitolium ascendere* (for which expression cf. also Pliny, *Paneg. Trai.* 23.4) when undertaken by Christians was synonymous with apostasy. [The term *Capitolini*, however, was not given so much to apostates themselves (thus the German translator J. Baer in a note to the present passage) as applied in scorn by the heretical Novatians to the church in Africa for not refusing reconciliation to its apostates (cf. Pacian, *Ep.* 2: PL 13.1059A).] See A. Hermann (for †F. J. Dölger), 'Capitolium,' RAC 2 (1954) 847–61.

35 *eorum* for *suus*. Such interchanges were common in the popular language; they are very rare in Cyprian—cf. LCP 5.154. But it may

be explained here because 'their *doom*' is not what *they* thought it, but what Cyprian calls it.

[36] 'come to the Capitol'—cf. above, n. 34.

[37] 'altar of the devil': *diaboli altare*. In the previous sentence 'altar' stands for *ara*, used by Cyprian of heathen altars only. *Altare* is the Christian altar: his use of the word here with *diaboli* (as in *Ep.* 59.12— a similar context) underlines the sacrilege (qualifying Watson 268, 288).

[38] *velut funus et bustum vitae suae.*

[39] In those days even infants received Communion; cf. the incident graphically described below in ch. 25.

[40] Isa. 52.11. 'Break away': *separamini*, following the LXX; Vulg. *mundamini*: 'be ye clean' (Douay).—'carry': *fertis*. That this was Cyprian's reading is clear from the text here and from Hartel's apparatus at *Test.* 3.34 (where, in the text, A's reading *portatis* is given); cf. *De unit.* 24 and n. 190.

[41] Apoc. 18.4.

[42] Cf. Matt. 10.23 and John 7.2; 8.59; 10.39. Cyprian gives the reasons for his own withdrawal in *Ep.* 20.1.

[43] 'withdraws': *cedere*, i.e. into voluntary exile.

[44] Cf. Gen. 3.14.

[45] 'the things of earth': *terrestribus*, rare for *terrenis* (Watson 287), but probably here chosen for the rhythm.

[46] Matt. 19.21. 'all thou hast': *omnia tua*. So too *De opere et eleemosynis* 7, and probably *Test.* 3.1 (where *bona tua* is also attested); Vulg. *quae habes*. Von Soden says (95) that both the former are African, and himself prefers the second—which is surprising as both MS e and Tertullian give *omnia tua*.—'the poor': *pauperibus* with Vulg. The usual African text has *egenis*, which the better MSS read in *Test.* 3.1 and *De op. et el.* 7 (cf. below, ch. 12 and n. 48). Here, for once, Cyprian allowed his natural preference to get the better of his usual fidelity to the written word. He never uses *egenus* spontaneously, but *pauper* (von Soden, 73, 98 n.); cf. below ch. 20 and n. 98 (cf. Matzkow, *in loc.*).

[47] *sub apostolis*; cf. above, ch. 6 and n. 18.

[48] 1 Tim. 6.9 f. 'snares,' literally, 'mousetraps': *muscipula* (Vulg. *laqueum*). The same word is used at *Test.* 3.61, *De dominica oratione* 19, and *De op. et el.* 10, quoting the same text. Both feminine and neuter, singular and plural are found in the MSS. Von Soden (88 f.) considers the neuter plural to be the original. The word occurs only once in the Vulgate—Wisd. 14.11. Cf. Rönsch, 218 f., and Blaise-Chirat, *s.v.*— 'erred': *erraverunt* with Vulg. This is one of several instances where *De laps.* presents a Scripture text different from that current in Africa. In *Dom. orat.* 19 and *De op. et el.* 10 the only reading is *naufragaverunt*;

in *Test.* 3.61 Hartel quotes only one MS with *erraverunt*. Martin here reads *naufragaverunt* with V (alone); but it is the reading also of one of the old Oxford MSS—cf. JTS 32 (1931) 424; von Soden 98 n.

⁴⁹ Luke 18.29; also quoted by Cyprian in *Test.* 3.16, *Ad Fortunatum* 12, and *Ep.* 58.2.—'or land': not in the Greek, but no doubt borrowed from Matt. 19.29 or Mark 10.30 (*aut agros*).—'seven times': *septies* (also read in MS e). Actually Luke has 'many times more': *multo plura* (Vulg.). Matthew and Mark have 'a hundred times more.' The simplest explanation is that of a double false 'aural reminiscence': *centies* being remembered as *septies*, and then included in the Luke quotation as if it were that of Mark (where *centies* is found in most O.L. MSS). For parallels in St. Augustine, cf. C. H. Milne, *A Reconstruction of the Old-Latin Text or Texts of the Gospels used by St. Augustine* (Cambridge 1926) 112.

⁵⁰ Luke 6.22 f. 'as evil': *ut nequam*; Vulg. *tamquam malum*. Elsewhere Cyprian uses *quasi* in quoting this passage (*Test.* 3.16; *Ad Fort.* 12; *Ep.* 58.2). See above, n. 48.

⁵¹ *sacramenti mei memor*; cf. above, ch. 7 n. 28. The military imagery of the passage leaves no doubt as to the meaning of *sacramentum* here.

⁵¹ᵃ The martyrs Castus and Aemilius were to be kept in high honour in Christian Africa (feast, May 22). St. Augustine's Sermon 285 is given to them. See T. Ruinart, *Acta Martyrum* (Regensburg 1859) 248.

⁵² *ad precem satisfactionis*. This introduces the real theme of his address: the necessity on the part of the lapsed of making satisfaction. But from the first Cyprian makes it a matter of hope and encouragement.

⁵³ Isa. 3.12; cf. *Test.* 3.115 and *Ep.* 34.2.

⁵⁴ Apoc. 3.19.

⁵⁵ 'infected parts': *putraminibus*. The first appearance of this word. Cyprian uses it again in *Ep.* 59.15 (where *colliganda* is suggested for *colligenda*, Watson 302). Cf. Souter, Blaise-Chirat, *s.v.*

⁵⁶ 'a new source of disaster': Cyprian had first denounced it in *Ep.* 15.

⁵⁷ *sub misericordiae titulo*: cf. *De unit.* 3 and n. 16.

⁵⁸ 'certain people': *quorundam*. Here and elsewhere in this address, Cyprian avoids a direct mention of those whom he has to criticize. His vague references were clear enough to his hearers, if not always to us. In this case he is obviously aiming at those priests who were reconciling the lapsed without previous penance (cf. *Ep.* 15.1, 43.3, etc.).

⁵⁹ 'readmission to communion is being granted': *laxatur . . . communicatio*. *Laxare* here takes on the meaning of 'opening up.' Cyprian uses it again four times in *Ep.* 55: §3 (with *pax*), 19 (with *communicatio*), 20 (with *paenitentia*, twice). Watson 308: 'I can find no parallel';

but Souter, *s.v.*, 'Cyp. on'; cf. also Blaise-Chirat, *s.v.*, so too H. Koch, *Cyprianische Untersuchungen* (Bonn 1926) 266–68, who gives many examples.

[60] For the necessity of doing thorough penance before reconciliation, cf. below, ch. 17, with the relevant notes. So far is the present passage from supporting the view that Cyprian then held that the greater sins could not be forgiven at all by the Church, that it really implies that they could. To condemn overhaste in granting reconciliation (cf. next chapter) is not to deny its being eventually granted; rather it implies it.

[61] 'Our Lord's sacred body': *sanctum Domini*; so too below, ch. 26 (twice). Cf. in *De unit.* 8 the pleonastic *caro Christi et sanctum Domini* (Watson 266).

[62] 'reeking': *infectis nidore*. Up to the 9th century the communicant received the Eucharist in his hand.

[63] Lev. 7.19 f. Cyprian's text follows the LXX closely, except that the Greek ascribes the 'saving,' not the 'sacrifice,' to the Lord.—Vulg. and Douay avoid the awkward 'and his own defilement be upon him,' by beginning the sentence simply with: '*Anima polluta . . .*': 'If anyone that is defiled. . . .'

[64] 1 Cor. 10.21.

[65] 1 Cor. 11.27.

[66] 'open acknowledgment': *exhomologesin*. This word had both a general sense, that of 'confessing' (e.g. praising God with or without reference to human sinfulness—as in *Test.* 3.114 and in ch. 31 [cf. n. 153], where Dan. 3.25 is quoted) or unburdening the conscience (as in ch. 28 [cf. n. 142]), and a technical sense, standing for one essential part of the penitential process. This came at the end of the period of penance, being a public act of humiliation, when bishop, priests, and faithful satisfied themselves as to the penitent's conduct since his fall (a detailed 'public confession,' however, was not exacted). The bishop (and priests) would then 'impose hands' with prayer and blessing, after which the penitent was readmitted to the ranks of the faithful at Communion. So *Ep.* 17.2: 'Penance must be done during the appropriate period, and the open acknowledgment (*exhomologesis*) must be made, with a scrutiny of the penitent's conduct, and finally no one can be received back to Communion until the bishop and his clergy have imposed hands upon him'; cf. *Ep.* 16.2, quoted above, Introd. n. 4. That the laity too had their part in the reconciliation is shown e.g. in *Ep.* 64.1 and 59.15.—Circumstances might prevent the *exhomologesis* being 'public,' e.g. in case of sickness, *Ep.* 18.1, 19.2. See K. Rahner, *art. cit.*, ZKT 74 (1952) 258–60.

⁶⁷ 'sacrifice . . . or imposition of his hands.' This refers to the Church's co-operation with the sinner's acts of penitence: Masses offered on his behalf, and prayers said over him as he acknowledges his guilt; see Rahner, *ibid.* 404 f. and 274 n. 23.

⁶⁸ 'the *pax*.' Reconciliation with the Church is meant (cf. Blaise-Chirat, *s.v.* 9); the word is here left untranslated because of what follows.

⁶⁹ 'certain men': *quidam*. The same as those referred to in the previous chapter (n. 58). So 'those men' in the next sentence.

⁷⁰ 'hawking about': *venditant*. In *Ep.* 15.3 he refers to them as those *qui personas accipientes in beneficiis vestris* (i.e. of the 'confessors') *aut gratificantur aut inlicitae negotiationis nundinas aucupantur*; cf. *Ep.* 17.2 *nisi illos quidam de presbyteris gratificantes decepissent*, and *Ep.* 34.1 *adulatione corrupta*.

⁷¹ 'sacrilege . . . sacrament': *impietatem . . . pietatis*. Such word-play is frequent with Cyprian.

⁷² Note how Cyprian implies the necessity of reconciliation with the Church for salvation. The invalidity of the 'reconciliation' in this case was not only due to the absence of adequate penance, but also to the disregard for Cyprian's episcopal rulings in the matter. Thus in *Ep.* 64.1, a reconciliation before the penance had been completed is nevertheless regarded as valid (though illicit), because granted by the bishop concerned.

⁷³ 'the crafty Enemy': *subtilis inimicus*. Disliking Greek words, Cyprian has several alternatives for *diabolus*. Thus *De unit.* 1 has *hostis, adversarius, inimicus, serpens*, all within ten lines (cf. Watson 285 f.). That passage and most of *De unit.* 3 are developments of the idea outlined here, but applied to schism.

⁷⁴ Apoc. 2.5; cf. *Ep.* 19.1 and 34.1. in a similar context.

⁷⁵ 'mercy.' For a full discussion of the problems raised by chs. 17–20, cf. M. Bévenot, 'The Sacrament of Penance and St. Cyprian's *De lapsis*,' *Theol. Stud.* 16 (1955) 175–213, where the explanations given in the notes here are substantiated.

⁷⁶ 'cancelled': *veniam largiri*, i.e. punishment as well as offence forgiven—as in baptism. Cyprian is not denying the Church's power to forgive sins; he is denouncing the action of those priests who were dispensing with all 'satisfaction,' allowing the lapsed to come to Communion without exacting any penance from them at all.

⁷⁷ 'Man cannot be above God.' Those priests claimed that the martyrs had *remitted* the sins of all the lapsed. Cyprian says that that puts the martyrs on a level with God, and makes the lapsed trust in the martyrs in place of God.

[78] 'that he knows not': *si nesciat*. *Si* here has the force of the Greek εἰ (for ὅτι); cf. LCP 6.115.

[79] Jer. 17.5; cf. *Test.* 3.10.

[80] 'It is the Lord. . . .' Those priests were saying: 'No need for satisfaction.' Cyprian reminds the lapsed of Our Lord's threat against those who denied Him; their only hope is to try to win Him over by personal penance, such as was then performed under the guidance of the bishop. When that was completed, Christ would forgive them, for the bishop was commissioned by Christ to act as judge in His place. The bishop, as priest of God, is 'judge, here and now, deputizing for Christ': *ad tempus iudex vice Christi* (*Ep.* 59.5). By by-passing the bishop's authority, the laxists were 'overriding Our Lord's commands' (ch. 18—cf. n. 85a), i.e. the Church's discipline and constitution as Christ had laid it down.

[81] Cf. Matt. 10.33, already referred to above in ch. 7.

[82] Cf. John 5.22.

[83] 'the merits of the martyrs.' Cyprian had the highest regard for the martyrs and recognized the right of those who had suffered for the faith to intercede for those of the fallen who had given proof of sincere repentance. In ch. 20 he shows that the martyrs would be contradicting themselves if they sanctioned (as those priests asserted that they did) the wholesale condonation of the lapsed, making even contrition superfluous. Therefore the priests could not justly claim to be carrying out the wishes of the martyrs. But here, with ch. 18, he makes up an artificial argument—perhaps jokingly—based on the quotation from the Apocalypse: 'How long, O Lord, etc.' In St. John's vision the martyrs are seen at the foot of the heavenly altar praying to be avenged. Well, they will be avenged at the end of the world; so, till then, they are in no position to be acting as judges, let alone giving decisions in opposition to the Supreme Judge. Any message they may have left is subject to the judgment of the bishop (cf. above, n. 80), who will decide whether it is in conformity with Christ's decrees or not.—The artificiality of the argument (which is quite in keeping with the rhetorical character of this address to his flock) is clear enough. Taken quite literally it would contradict Cyprian's well-known esteem for the martyrs, and above all it would imply that repentant sinners had to wait for the last day before they reached heaven. In fact, he repeatedly speaks of the martyrs as receiving their crown *at once*, and of the rest of the faithful as joining their loved ones at death, in the happiness of heaven; e.g. *Ad Fort.* 12 f.; *De mort.* 17, 26; etc.

[84] 'the passing of this present world': *occasum saeculi huius et mundi*.

Both words stand for 'the world,' the first being the more common; for the pleonasm, cf. Watson 287. Cyprian does not distinguish between the particular and the general judgments; he insists on the fact of judgment, not on its date.

85 'anyone,' i.e. of the laxist priests.

85a Cf. M. Bévenot, *art. cit.*, *Theol. Stud.* 16 (1955) 200–203. Also above, n. 80.

86 'His decree,' that is, as stated in Matt. 10.32 f., just referred to (in part), in ch. 17 (cf. n. 81) and earlier (in full) in ch. 7 (cf. n. 33). Cyprian quotes and comments on it fully below, ch. 20.

87 'God's altar': *ara Dei*. Except when, as here, Cyprian is reproducing Apoc. 6.9, he uses *ara* of pagan altars only. For the Christian altar he uses *altare*, a much less common word, and perhaps for that reason more often adopted by the Christians; cf. above, ch. 8 and n. 37.

88 Apoc. 6.10.

89 'Is it credible, then . . .'—a very complicated sentence, so that one might suspect a corruption of the text.

90 'Suppose . . .'—a highly ironical passage. He has just proved that the martyrs are in no position to issue reprieves; he now adopts an attitude of deference to their behests—in imitation of the laxists—but exacts a little humility from the petitioning sinners, a virtue in which they were notoriously deficient.—During the persecution, Cyprian had appealed to the 'martyrs' and confessors to observe moderation and circumspection in the recommendations for reconciliation which they addressed to him (*Ep.* 15.3 f.). They must know the penitents personally and testify that the penance which they have so far done is close to being fully adequate: *quos nostis, quorum paenitentiam satisfactioni proximam conspicitis* (*Ep.* 15.4).

91 The end of ch. 20 shows (n. 101) that this is merely a supposition, to round off his argument.

92 Exod. 32.31–33. After 'grievous crime,' the omission of 'and they have made to themselves gods of gold' is not due to a lacuna in Cyprian's Bible; he quotes the complete text in three other places.—'And now if Thou wouldst forgive them their crime, forgive them; but if not . . .': a literal translation of the LXX, closely reproducing the Hebrew idiom (which, however, omits the second 'forgive them'). Vulg. makes the sense clear: '*aut dimitte eis hanc noxam, aut si non facis,* 'Either forgive them this trespass, or, if thou do not, . . .' (Douay).—'him will I strike out': *deleam*, instead of *delebo* (Vulg.). The present subjunctive was at times used with a future sense, especially in the second conjugation, cf. LCP 6.19; 9.85–87; many examples in Rönsch 290 f.—This passage of Exod., because quoted by so many early authors, is important for comparing the different forms of the O.L.; cf. A. V. Billen, *The Old Latin Texts of the Heptateuch* (Cambridge 1927) 41–43.

[93] Jer. 1.5. 'Unto the nations.' Hartel here prints *in gentes* (LXX), though *in gentibus* seems more likely—cf. *Test.* 1.21.

[94] Jer. 11.14, following the LXX. 'Ask not for them in prayer and petition': *noli postulare pro eis in prece et oratione*; Vulg.: *ne assumas pro eis laudem et orationem*: 'do not take up praise and prayer for them' (Douay).

[95] 'constancy in the faith more robust': *quid . . . in fidei firmitate robustius?* Both here and repeatedly in the following lines, *in* is used for the plain ablative of respect, according to the general tendency of the time to visualize, and then to describe by the most appropriate preposition; cf. LCP 5.113–16, 123; 9.64 f.; also *De unit.* 3 and n. 16.

[95a] 'and won,' i.e. by his 'constancy in the faith.'—'survived unscathed,' i.e. through the 'favour of God.'

[96] Ezech. 14.13 f., 18.

[97] Cf. *Ep.* 30.7: *et qui petitur flecti debet, non incitari, et sicut respici debet divina clementia, sic respici debet et divina censura*, etc. (from Rome).

[98] Matt. 10.32 f.; the text which dominates Cyprian's thought throughout his handling of the lapsed.—A small but perhaps significant textual problem appears here. In the four other passages where Cyprian quotes this text (*Test.* 3.16; *Ad Fort.* 5; *Ep.* 12.1; 16.2), we read *confessus fuerit in me*, the ordinary 'African' reading, whereas here we have *confessus me fuerit*. Von Soden (98 n., cf. 95) calls attention to several such differences precisely in the *De lapsis*, and raises the question, though hesitantly, whether in the text-transmission, its Scripture quotations have not been revised according to a 'European version.' But he admits that, if so, it was not thorough-going. In any case, the *De laps.* accompanied the *De unit.*, which shows no sign of such a revision. For the two main versions, cf. Matzkow *in loc.*

[99] As is implied by those who receive back the lapsed without any penance.

[100] 'shall . . . receive': *accipiunt*. Cyprian very often uses the present for the future, especially when he is propounding truths of the faith, e.g. above, *si negantem non negat, nec confitentem confitetur*. So *De unit.* 6 (n. 50); 14 (n. 111). It is the application to the certainties of faith of a construction not uncommon for emphasizing a general truth, as for instance in *De unit.* 5 (n. 46); cf. LCP 9.72–79.

[101] This defence of the good name of the martyrs shows that the passage at the end of ch. 18 was merely a supposition, and that Cyprian did not really think that the martyrs had been so presumptuous. This

is significant. For he had originally been prepared to blame the martyrs at least for the recommendations made *gregatim multis* (*Ep.* 27.1), and then *semel cunctis* (27.3), as tending to force his hand, since it would create *invidiam verecundiae nostrae* if he refused any of those so recommended (*ibid.* and *Ep.* 27.2). But, since then, a letter from Rome had suggested a more kindly interpretation: the 'martyrs' had perhaps themselves only yielded to the force of importunities and, after all, *they* had not claimed to forgive of themselves but had referred their clients to the bishop (*Ep.* 36.2). Cyprian's altered attitude in the *De lapsis* is governed by that letter from Rome.

[102] Cyprian here passes to a new subject, that the persecution was God's judgment on them for their sins—a fresh motive for the lapsed to do penance. The laxist priests (hinted at here) have ignored this—cf. Bévenot, *art. cit., Theol. Stud.* 16 (1955) 207 n. 116.

[103] *Nisi si*: expressing strong irony, as in Tertullian; cf. LCP 6.112 f., where many examples are given from Cyprian's letters.

[104] 'All these calamities': *omnia ista*. Perhaps a reminiscence of Our Lord's prophecy of the destruction of Jerusalem; cf. Mark 13.30: *donec omnia ista fiant.*

[105] 'stubborn': reading *indociles* with several MSS, in place of Hartel's choice, *indocibiles*, the unteachable. If the latter is correct, it is the first appearance of the word (Watson 304); Souter's *Glossary* lists it only from the 4th century on.

[106] Isa. 42.24 f., following LXX. 'the fury of His wrath': *iram animationis suae.* An unusual meaning for the word *animatio* (Vulg. reads *furoris*), but found in several Christian writers (cf. TLL 1 *s.v.* fin.; Blaise-Chirat, *s.v.* 2). The passage is quoted again in *De dom. orat.* 25.—It is from Scriptural phrases of this kind that Merkx (LCP 9.12-15) explains the frequency in Christian Latin authors of the *genetivus inhaerentiae*, a poetical or rhetorical pleonasm in which both words have the same meaning (cf. LCP 5.81-85). There are many examples in Cyprian; e.g. above, ch. 7, 'the wrath of the divine displeasure': *iram divinae indignationis*; *De unit.* 5, 'by the copiousness of its welling waters': *exundantis copiae largitate*; *ibid.*, 'in generous growth': *copia ubertatis*; 9, 'concord and peace': *concordiam pacis*; 17, 'for his reckless insolence': *ob temeritatis audaciam*, etc.

[107] Isa. 59.1 f., following the LXX with the first sentence interrogative.—'dulled': *gravavit*, lit. 'made heavy.' In *Test.* 2.4 and 3.47, and in *Ad Demetr.* 11, Hartel prints *gravabit* against the preponderance of MSS; here he keeps *gravavit* with the LXX (cf. Martin, *ad loc.*).

[108] *servare voluisse.* One might translate simply, 'we have never obeyed.' For Cyprian sometimes uses *velle, coepisse* pleonastically, and

voluisse provides him with a good rhythmical ending, impossible with *servasse* (cf. LCP 6.49, and below, *De unit.* n. 203); see E. De Jonge, *Les clausules métriques dans Saint Cyprien* (Louvain-Paris 1905) 45 (present clausula listed).

[109] 'sacred ministers . . . sacrilege': *sacerdotibus . . . sacrilegus*. Cyprian likes to bring *sacerdos* into contact with its cognates by way of contrast. Another favourite instance of this tendency is *fides* and *perfidia*; cf. *De unit.* 17 and n. 136; 21 and n. 177 (Watson 227, 289); or again *spes* and *desperatio*, cf. *De unit.* 3 and n. 20a. So too, below, *inplacabilis . . . placari*.

[110] 'those who are bishops and priests of God': *antistites et sacerdotes Dei*. Pleonastic; only those with episcopal rank being referred to (Watson 259); cf. ch. 26 and n. 132.

[111] 'so unrelentingly . . . moved to relent': *inplacabilis . . . placari*.

[112] 'already': *interim*, lit. 'in between whiles,' i.e. here, in the time up to the hour of death. *Interim* often presents difficulties of translation in Cyprian. Its most technical sense of 'during this life' comes from our 'not having here an abiding city'; it is the interval before our true life begins. But as it can mean 'any time in this life,' in contrast with the next, so may it even mean 'at once,' e.g. of the reconciliation of the *libellatici* (*Ep.* 55.17) in contrast with the long penance to be imposed on the *sacrificati*: cf. Watson 313 n. 3; P. Galtier, *L'église et la rémission des péchés* (Paris 1932) 292 f.; B. Poschmann, *Paenitentia secunda* (Bonn 1940) 383–90.

[113] 'The penalty of a few.' The examples given by Cyprian in the next three chapters may appear exaggerated. Of only one does he say that he saw it himself: the baby who choked when given Communion. Certainly he makes good use of such interventions of Providence to rouse his people to the fear of God. Perhaps they tell us more of the mentality of his flock than of himself. Note that he is emphasizing throughout the sacredness of the Eucharist and the sacrilege committed by unworthy reception, and not, for instance, any guilt on the part of the baby—any more than he had done in ch. 9.

[114] 'went up to the Capitol'; cf. ch. 8, nn. 34, 36.

[115] 'with which to beg for mercy': *ad precum misericordiam*. If the text is correct, the thought seems to be 'to call down mercy upon the [offerer of] prayers [of sorrow],' *precum* being taken as an objective genitive.

[115a] The baths played an important part in the social life of the Roman Empire. Besides their utilitarian purpose, they provided the setting for exercise and physical culture, or simply for loitering and relaxation. The physical pleasure, which formed the predominant

attraction of the baths, is what Cyprian here (and still more below, ch. 30) denounces as incompatible with the spirit of penance which the lapsed should be cultivating. Besides, the mingling of the sexes at the baths, which under the circumstances was regarded even by pagans as indecent, often led to disorders, but even repeated imperial legislation was unable to check its popularity. Its vogue in Carthage is evidenced by Cyprian in *De hab. virg.* 19–21. On the whole question cf. J. Jüthner's article 'Bad' in RAC 1 (1950) 1134 ff.

[116] 'tasted and uttered': *vel pasta . . . vel locuta. Vel* for *et*, cf. ch. 6 and n. 19.

[117] 'by those who had already doomed themselves': *pereuntium.* But it may mean merely 'by the pagans'—cf. 1 Cor. 1.18.

[118] *sacrificantibus nobis,* cf. next chapter, with nn. 128, 131.

[119] 'this mischance occurred' (namely of intrusion or unlawful approach to the Eucharist): *obreptum est,* a word regularly used in this sense. So too at the beginning of the next chapter, *latenter obrepsit.* Those admitted were the *sancti:* 'in the midst of the faithful' (cf. next note).

[120] *cum sanctis.* Perhaps the only time that Cyprian so calls them (Watson and Janssen both miss it): he does so because of their being gathered to receive the Eucharist; cf. the priest's invitation '*Sancta sanctis*' in the Oriental rites (see J. A. Jungmann, *Missarum Sollemnia* [Vienna 1948] 2.2.3 ch. 3 nn. 22–29).

[121] 'the prayer and the offering': *precis nostrae et orationis.* Cyprian uses both terms for prayer for others, especially the series of prayers then said early in the Mass, of which we have an example on Good Friday. So *De dom. orat.* 8 and 17; *Ep.* 37.1; 62.5. *Oratio,* besides its general use, also stands specifically for the 'Canon' of the Mass; cf. *De dom. orat.* 31: *sacerdos ante orationem praefatione praemissa parat fratrum mentes dicendo 'Susum corda.'* Cf. below, *sollemnibus adinpletis,* n. 123; and *De unit.* 17 n. 138.

[122] *ploratu concuti.* As Cyprian reaches the climax of his story, he breaks into historic infinitives. So *iactari, avertere, premere, recusare,* all of the struggling infant.

[123] 'sacred rites': *sollemnibus adinpletis.* An alternative to *sacrificium* for describing the Mass, cf. ch. 26 and n. 131, and the title of J. A. Jungmann's monumental work, *Missarum Sollemnia.*

[124] *diaconus offerre.* It has sometimes been taken that this verb, when in a liturgical context, necessarily means 'to offer the sacrifice,' in some degree or other. It clearly cannot mean that here; the deacon is distributing the sacred elements to the people.

[125] 'some of the consecrated chalice': *de sacramento calicis.* The

meaning is clear, if the exact force of each word is not. Cf. Poukens, in de Ghellinck 217, and LCP 9.7, where *calicis* is taken as a *genetivus definitivus*.—The partitive *de*, without a preceding word denoting the part, is here unique in Cyprian, cf. LCP 9.31.

[126] 'sanctified by Our Lord's blood': *sanctificatus in Domini sanguine*. A 'local' *in* with strong instrumental force—cf. LCP 9.48. This characteristic use of *in* is analyzed in LCP 5.113–17.—R reads *sanguinem*, which would assert the transformation of the wine into the Precious Blood. But this is probably an over-zealous correction on behalf of orthodoxy. Cyprian's preoccupation is elsewhere. What was drunk was hallowed because steeped in Our Lord's blood (or because Our Lord's blood was steeped in it); no need here to underline what he and his readers knew well enough—cf. *Ep.* 63.

[127] 'priest': *sacerdos*, i.e. himself, Cyprian, the bishop.—The importance of this chapter and the next for the liturgical customs at Carthage at this time needs no underlining.

[128] 'those assisting at [our] sacrifice': *sacrificantibus*. The possibility that a pagan sacrifice is referred to throughout seems to be excluded by the phrase *latenter obrepsit*, which is out of place in any but a Christian setting; cf. nn. 118, 119, 131.

[129] 'the locket': the Eucharist might at times be taken home for private Communion; cf. also Novatian, *De spectaculis* 5; Tertullian, *Ad ux.* 2.5; *De or.* 19.

[130] 'Our Lord's holy body'; cf. above, ch. 15 with n. 61 and here, next sentence.

[131] 'sacrifice': *sacrificio*. 'The usual title for the Eucharistic service is *sacrificium*, either alone,' as here and *Ep.* 61.4, 'or more often *sacrificium divinum* or *dominicum*' (Watson 266).

[132] *a sacerdote*. The word expresses the bishop's sacrificial and mediatorial functions; *episcopus*, his hierarchical position. Cyprian never calls him *summus sacerdos*, as Tertullian does: '(*baptismum*) *dandi quidem habet ius summus sacerdos qui est episcopus; dehinc presbyteri et diaconi non tamen sine episcopi auctoritate*' (*De bapt.* 17). There is no passage in Cyprian where *sacerdos* must stand for *presbyter*; it normally stands for the bishop (so for the next two or three centuries). Watson (258 n.) finds only five passages where it might mean *presbyter*, giving reasons against. This might be taken as a sixth. (Cf. LCP 8.72 ff. and 82 ff. for a comparison with Tertullian's use.) But whether a *presbyter* was called *sacerdos* or not, there is no doubt about his saying Mass. This is clear from the letters in which Cyprian forbids his *presbyteri* to 'offer' on behalf of the lapsed or to give them Communion before their case has been properly gone into; he threatens them with suspension

if they do (cf. *Ep.* 15.1 and especially *Ep.* 16; so too *Ep.* 17.2; 31.6; 34.1,3).

[133] 'brings no blessing': *nec . . . ad salutem prodesse*; lit., 'does not benefit unto salvation.'

[134] 'the Holy One': *sancto.* It might also be translated: 'its holy character' or 'consecration' (Watson 266: 'either . . . *Christo* or . . . a neuter abstract'), but the context ('Our Lord removes Himself') seems against it. This presages the famous Medieval debate: what precisely does the sinner receive in Communion? Here, with the disappearance of the 'species,' it is clear that the Real Presence had gone.

[135] 'refusing . . . souls': omitted in many MSS, and only given by Hartel in his apparatus criticus. But its presence in V (which Hartel missed), the good sense which, superficially, remains in spite of its omission, yet the need of it here where Cyprian is summing up the lesson of his examples, all combine to show that it is original, but was early lost in some ancient archetype.

[135a] 'confession of apostasy': *professio denegantis*, cf. ch. 3 n. 14.

[136] Matt. 6.24.

[137] 'in the eyes of men': i.e. of the pagans, by making them think that he had sacrificed.

[138] Ps. 138 (Heb. 139).16. All three chief MSS of the LXX (BSA) read: '*My* eyes have seen *Thy* being as not made.' Hilary and Ambrose discuss a Latin version of this. But the version used by Cyprian and others (and now in Vulg.), shows that there was probably an alternative LXX reading (such as is found e.g. in the corrections here made in Sinaiticus).

[139] 1 Kings (1 Sam.) 16.7. 'upon the countenance': *in faciem*—as in LXX, εἰς πρόσωπον. Vulg. *ea quae parent*: 'those things that appear' (Douay).

[140] Apoc. 2.23.

[141] Jer. 23.23 f., as in the LXX. The Vulg. makes both sentences interrogative.—These verses follow those quoted in *De unit.* 11 (n. 92); they also occur in *Test.* 3.56 (where Hartel's text needs correcting) and *De dom. orat.* 4.

[142] 'manifest their conscience': *exhomologesin conscientiae faciant*, exactly equivalent to the preceding *aput sacerdotes Dei . . . confitentes.* Here *exhomologesis* implies the confession, at least in private, of the nature of the sin committed; cf. Poschmann, *Paenitentia secunda* 420. But one cannot deduce from this the existence of 'private confession' in the modern sense (cf. K. Rahner, *art. cit.*, ZKT 74 [1952] 437 f.). See also ch. 16 with n. 66.

[143] Gal. 6.7.

143a Mark 8.38. 'put to shame': *confundet*, Vulg. *confundetur* (which is not classical). MS k reads *confundetur*, and Cyprian may have written this in *Ep.* 63.15 (however, cf. Hartel's apparatus). Von Soden seems only to have noticed the deponent form (431, 126, 611). The other O.L. MSS are about equally divided (cf. Matzkow *in loc.*).

144 'and': *aut . . . aut* for *et . . . et.* So too in the next sentence; cf. above, ch. 6 and n. 19.

145 'through the neglect of reparation': *in neglecta satisfactione.* The ablative of cause is regularly replaced by *in* and the ablative with affective verbs (*laetari, gaudere, contristari,* etc.). This passage is one of the rare instances in Cyprian without such a verb; LCP 5.119; 9.58 f.

146 'confession': *confessio*, here, of the final act of the penitent before the imposition of hands and reconciliation. As a rule Cyprian used *exhomologesis* instead (cf. *Ep.* 55.17 and 29, parallels to this passage), perhaps because 'confessing *Christ*' had almost monopolized the services of *confessio*; cf. ch. 3 with n. 14; ch. 16—n. 66; ch. 31—n. 153 (Poschmann, *Paenitentia secunda* 418–22).—'can still be heard': cf. *Test.* 3.114; and often in the Letters.

147 '. . . granted through the priests': *satisfactio et remissio facta per sacerdotes.* By comparing this with *Ep.* 43.3, K. Rahner shows that the priests are to be understood as assisting the penitents to make their *satisfactio* 'plena,' in view of the *remissio* to be obtained (Rahner, *art. cit.*, ZKT 74 [1952] 382 with n. 4, and 404 f. with n. 38). However, what Cyprian here says goes further than that, and ascribes the forgiveness itself to the ministry of the priests. There is no real contradiction here with what he has said in ch. 17 (cf. nn. 75–80 and M. Bévenot, *art. cit.*, Theol. Stud. 16 [1955] 186 f. and 208, where, however, the text is translated in Rahner's sense).

148 Joel 2.12. 'along with': *simulque et. Simul* has practically the value of a preposition; cf. Rönsch 400; also LCP 6.71 for the combination *simul et.*

148a 'at the baths': cf. above, ch. 24 and n. 115a.

149 'those in need': *cum pauperum necessitate.* A trick of style, used by the poets, and affected by Cicero and Cyprian too: a genitive depending on an abstract noun, where, in the normal construction, the substantive in the genitive would take the case of the other, and the abstract would be its adjective, e.g. 'the necessitous poor'; cf. LCP 5.86 f. Other examples in *De unit.* 2 (n. 13); 14 (n. 121); 21 (n. 178). See LCP 9.17–19.

150 Lev. 19.27: *Non corrumpetis effigiem barbae vestrae,* following the LXX. *Effigies* (ὄψις) here simply means 'outward appearance' (TLL 5.2.183) Vulg. *nec radetis barbam*: 'nor [shall you] shave your beard' (Douay). Cf. *Test.* 3.84: *Non vellendum,* and above, ch. 6 and n. 22.

[151] 'the "putting on of Christ,"' which took place in baptism—see Gal 3.27 (cf. Rom. 13.14); cf. in a similar context: *sericum et purpuram indutae Christum induere non possunt (De hab. virg.* 13); and *De unit.* 7.

[152] 'eyes . . . kohl': *nigri pulveris ductu oculorum lineamenta depingis.* The context suggests a reference to Jer. 4.30.—On dyeing the hair and making up generally, cf. *De hab. virg.* 14–17. Cyprian was a rigorist in the matter, and perhaps circumstances demanded such a line. But the high spiritual motives behind his attitude have not lost their force to-day.

[153] 'making confession to God.' Cyprian is commenting on Dan. 3.25 (which he is about to quote), and gives to the word *exhomologesis* a penitential sense, which is justified by the context, though in the original the sense of 'praise' predominates (Watson 290 n. 2). Cf. ch. 16 with n. 66.

[154] 'earned God's favour': *Dominum . . . promeriti. Promerere(-i) aliquem* in the sense of 'winning someone over' can be paralleled in a number of authors from Ovid onwards, cf. Heb. 13.16 (Vulg.); Rönsch 377; H. Koch, *Cyprianische Untersuchungen* (Bonn 1926) 316 f. Cf. below: *(Daniel) adhuc promereri Deum nititur:* 'continued to strive after God's favour,' and ch. 32, *in promerenda Dei maiestate;* also *De unit.* 15 and n. 124; 18 and n. 148.

[155] 'tortures': *inter ipsa gloriosa virtutum suarum martyria.* But as in fact they were protected from the effect of the flames, Cyprian may not have meant 'tortures,' but simply 'in the midst of the glory which testified to their virtues.' However, the glory of *martyrdom* cannot have been alien to his thought even here. Watson (290) calls *martyria* here and in *Ep.* 61.4 'otiose.'

[156] Dan. 3.25. The details of the text show that it depends on the LXX. But by the time of St. Jerome, the Church was using Theodotion's version as being far more faithful to the original; (the Aramaic of Dan. 3.24–90 is missing).—'Made confession to God': *exhomologesin faciebat Deo.'* The words, for the sake of which Cyprian quoted the passage, occur in the LXX but not in Theodotion (nor Vulg., etc.).— The Biblical accounts of Daniel in the lions' den and the three youths in the fiery furnace were constantly drawn upon in patristic literature and ancient Christian painting (catacombs).

[157] Dan. 9.4–7 (cf. preceding note). The dependence on the LXX is very clear: 'we have not listened to what Thy children the Prophets have spoken': *non audivimus puerorum tuorum prophetarum quae locuti sunt.* Though the Greek genitive, here reproduced, is common to both

Greek versions, *quae* represents & in the LXX in opposition to οἱ in Theodotion (Vulg. *qui*, as also Augustine). The Hebrew of this part of Daniel is preserved.

158 The force of Cyprian's appeals was enhanced by the way that he identified himself with the needs of his people; cf. chs. 4 and 22. Here, besides, he assures the lapsed of the sympathy and help of all the others.

159 Isa. 29.10: *et dedit illis Deus spiritum transpunctionis*; lit., 'God hath given them a spirit of transfixion.' Also quoted thus in *Ep.* 59.13. Vulg.: *quoniam miscuit vobis Deus spiritum soporis*: 'the Lord hath mingled for you the spirit of deep sleep.' St. Paul had quoted the passage from the LXX in Rom. 11.8, where the Vulg. reads *dedit illis spiritum compunctionis*. The Greek word, κατάνυξις, implies pricking, stabbing, piercing, the corresponding verb being used in Acts 2.37 (Peter's audience were 'pricked at heart'—Westminster Version). The Hebrew, however, used a different metaphor, that of a sleepy stupefaction, represented by *soporis* above, and suggested by Douay at Rom. 11.8 (in spite of *compunctionis* in the Vulg.!). Cf. Cornelius a Lapide on Rom. 11.8, who quotes Cyprian's comment here and in *Ep.* 59.13. But in both cases he makes Cyprian apply the quotation to the Jews, whereas in fact it was the obdurate *lapsi* whom he had in mind.

160 2 Thess. 2.10 f. 'the love of the truth': *dilectum veritatis*: Vulg. *caritatem*; Greek, ἀγάπην.—'shall send him.' *Mittet* was probably Cyprian's reading; it is that preferred in the Vulgate editions. Hartel gives only one MS for his choice of *mittit*, his favourite S, clinching it by referring to the Greek πέμπει, which, amazingly, he ascribes to the LXX! His other MSS (W and R) read *mittet*, to which Martin adds his M. [It is unfortunate that Martin should have so designated the Munich MS, Lat. 4597 (von Soden's 41), when for over eighty years M has stood for another Munich MS, namely Lat. 208 (von Soden's 40).]—This and the previous text are quoted and developed in *Ep.* 59.13, where even Hartel reads *mittet*.

161 Cf. 1 Cor. 10.12.

162 'reconciliation': *pacem*.

163 Cf. 17 (n. 79).

164 . . . at the moment of their 'lapse.'

165 'canker'; so too in *De unit.* 10. Cf. 2 Tim. 2.17, quoted in *Test.* 3.78 and *Ep.* 59.20. There is the same general warning in *De unit.* 17 with other Scriptural backing.

166 'catching': *transilit*. This seems to be a technical medical term, used, for instance, by Seneca in much the same way that Cyprian

does. He asks concerning men who want to make one think one is unhappy: 'Quid est quod trepident, quod contagium quoque mei timeant, quasi transilire calamitas possit?' (Seneca, Ep. 13.6).

[167] 'will be appeased': posse placari; cf. De unit. 20 and n. 165.

[168] 'whose temple etc.' The Christian's body was the temple of God (cf. 1 Cor. 3.16 f.; 2 Cor. 6.19; etc.), defiled by his communion in the idolatrous sacrifice—cf. above, ch. 10.

[169] 'Do you think that He will easily have mercy on you?': putas facile eum misereri tui? The present infinitive, with future meaning, is classical only after verbs of promising and the like. Here the freer use is exemplified, there being a plausible excuse for it in the ungainly alternative miserturum esse; LCP 9.80.—As for the thought, it may be that at one time Cyprian held that there was no forgiveness possible for apostasy (cf. Test. 3.28: 'There is no forgiveness in the Church for one who sins against God'). If so, his mind had by now changed: forgiveness is not given ʲacile, that is all. Cf. Ad Fortun. 4, and M. Bévenot, art. cit., Theol. Stud. 16 (1955) 188–91.

[170] 'good deeds': iustis operibus. One of several expressions in this chapter and the next to describe acts of charity and especially almsdeeds. Its origin may have been Matt. 6.1, where some Greek MSS read ἐλεημοσύνην for δικαιοσύνην, and elemosinam is found in the O.L. versions. But, for Cyprian, the part played by good works in the formation of the 'just' or perfect man was suggested not perhaps by James 2.24 (an epistle which he never quotes), but by such Old Testament passages as he cites in the treatise devoted to the subject, De opere et eleemosynis, e.g. in ch. 2: Prov. 15.27; Ecclus. 3.33; and in ch. 5: Dan. 4.24; Tob. 12.8 f. He clearly had this last text in mind here: Eleemosyna a morte liberat et ipsa purgat peccata (cf. H. Pétré, Caritas [Louvain 1948] 246–48). Such good works are also called by him opera salutaria in the same sense, and steeped as he was in Pauline theology he had no inhibitions about giving a large place to the doctrine of satisfaction, for which he is so strongly criticized by Archbishop E. W. Benson, Cyprian, his Life, his Times, his Work, (London 1897) 248 f.

[171] 'your largess be . . ., without stint': largiter fiat operatio. Both words (and their cognates) belong to the vocabulary of Christian charity. Largitio etc. in Cicero points merely to the size of the gift; in so far as it has any moral connotation, this is generally of a pejorative kind (arrogant or interested display). Used already by Tertullian in the Christian sense of almsdeeds, it figures freely in Cyprian in its many forms with all the implications of large-hearted generosity; so, below, 'they gave at once, and generously': prompti erant, largi erant.

Cf. Pétré, *op. cit.* 177 f., 191–93.—*Operatio* is a specially good example of a word which took on a new meaning in Christian circles. (As has been well pointed out, the modern word 'operation' takes on various specific senses according to the professional circle in which it is used. It differs in the hospital; in the army; on the Stock Exchange; in the mathematics class.) The genesis of the Christian sense of 'works of charity' was somewhat as follows: *Bona opera*, coming from Jewish tradition, has its place in the New Testament, and the Christians naturally used the term for almsdeeds. We have seen above Cyprian's use of *opera iusta* (or *opera iustitiae*); he also calls them *opera misericordiae* after Tertullian, who also inaugurated *opera dilectionis* and *opera caritatis*. This constant use made possible the abbreviation *opera* (plur.), the singular collective *opus* (cf. LCP 5.48), and the general abstract *operatio*, all used, without need of specification, for acts of charity in general and alsmdeeds in particular. (So in 'Catholic Action' circles, the word 'action' can stand by itself without fear of misunderstanding.) Besides the present passage, cf. above, ch. 6 with n. 21, *non in operibus misericordia*; *De unit.* 26 with n. 197, *largitas operationis*; *ibid.*, n. 201, *in Dei timore, in lege iustitiae, in dilectione, in opere fides nulla est*; and the title of his treatise *De opere et eleemosynis*, where the two words are synonymous. So below, ch. 36, we have the verb *operari* in the same sense: 'Towards sorrow, *good works*, pleadings . . .': *paenitenti, operanti, roganti. . . .* Cf. Pétré, *op. cit.* 240–63.—The development of charitable practices since the time of Tertullian is reflected in Cyprian's freer use of these terms. *Iustus*, meaning 'good' in the sense of 'charitable': *operans*, for 'a generous man'; *opus*, collectively for 'good works,' are not so used by Tertullian. Cf. LCP 8.215–24.

172 'to make Our Lord beholden to us': *Dominus faeneretur*. A clear reference to Prov. 19.17 (O.L.): *qui miseretur pauperi, Dominum faenerat*. Vulg. uses the deponent form and the dative: *faeneratur Domino, qui miseretur pauperis*, which, exceptionally, is closer to the LXX than is the O.L. Cyprian's reading of the verse is also illustrated by *De hab. virg.* 11, *patrimonio tuo Deum faenera*, and *De op. et el.* 16, *Deus eleemosynis pauperum faeneratur*. These should suffice, in the conflict of MSS, to restore the reading in *De dom. orat.* 33, and *De op. et el.* 15: *qui miseretur pauperi, Deum faenerat*; (Hartel prints *Deo* in both cases). Cf. TLL 6, *s.v. faenero*, 477 lines 54–58, 15–17.

173 'yet': *et*, for *sed*, as an emphatic adversative. 'The most noteworthy and almost the most common of Cyprian's usages [of conjunctions]' (Watson 315).

174 'to such He can extend His mercy': *misereri talium potest. Potest* in no way implies any doubt of God's forgiveness. After repeatedly

stressing Christ's threat against those who deny Him, Cyprian says that that does not mean He *cannot* forgive them. There is no cause for despair. The texts proclaiming His mercy show that He *can* be merciful, and will be, to those who fulfil the Church's penance. Nor is there any reason for separating God's forgiveness from the reconciliation with the Church, as if the latter were only something provisional. Cf. M. Bévenot, *art. cit., Theol. Stud.* 16 (1955) 210–13.

[175] Here, and later against Novatian (*Ep.* 55.22), Cyprian uses Tertullian's pre-Montanist teaching and Scriptural evidences for God's forgiveness. Cf. C. B. Daly, 'Novatian and Tertullian,' in *Irish Theol. Quart.* 19 (1952) 43.

[176] Isa. 30.15: *Cum conversus [fueris et] gemueris, tunc salvaberis et scies ubi fueris*; [*fueris et* to be deleted; cf. *Ep.* 34.1 and Hartel's apparatus here]. This reproduces the LXX. Vulg. follows the Heb.: *Si revertamini et quiescatis, salvi eritis; in silentio et in spe erit fortitudo vestra*: 'If you return and be quiet, you shall be saved. In silence and in hope shall your strength be' (Douay).—*Gemueris* (LXX στενάξῃς) suggests that √nuh in the Heb. was misread as √'nḥ.—No explanation suggests itself for the extraordinary *et scies ubi fueris*.

[177] *Nolo mortem morientis, dicit Dominus, quantum ut revertatur et vivat.* The same occurs in *De bon. pat.* 4. It begins with Ezech. 18.32 and continues with either Ezech. 18.23 or 33.11, all three passages expressing the same fundamental idea. In *Test.* 3.114 Cyprian quotes it in another form: *Malo peccatoris paenitentiam quam mortem*, which occurs in Pacian, *Ep.* 3.8: PL 13.1068D.

[178] Joel 2.13: *et qui sententiam flectat adversus malitias inrogatam*; [*malitias* (for *malitiam*) has better MS support here and in *De bono pat.* 4, and in *Ep.* 55.22]. Vulg.: *et praestabilis super malitia*; LXX: καὶ μετανοῶν ἐπὶ ταῖς κακίαις. What Vulg. means is not clear; (Douay: 'ready to repent of the evil'). LXX here agrees with Heb., and Cyprian's text is a free paraphrase.

[179] The action of the bishops (and priests) refers to the part played (*fecerint*) by the Church authorities in what then corresponded to the Sacrament of Penance.

[180] 'draws from the bitterness of his fall a fresh fund . . .': *plus . . . de ipso lapsus sui dolore conceperit*. An instrumental *de*, with a strong connotation of origin, so as almost to be equivalent to *ex*; cf. LCP 9.46.

THE UNITY OF THE CATHOLIC CHURCH

[1] Matt. 5.13.

[2] Cf. Matt. 10.16.

[3] Cf. 1 Cor. 1.24.

[4] 'for the care of our souls': lit. 'in preserving our [spiritual] health.' *Salus*, generally represented by 'salvation' in Christian literature, means originally 'health' of body, and then, of mind or soul. Perfect 'health of soul' for the Christian comes only in the next life; there are various degrees of it, i.e. of the state of grace, in this world. It is a pity that 'salvation' should have come to mean 'not being lost,' and that 'being in a state of grace' should be regarded as satisfactory because it means 'not being in mortal sin.' That is why *in tuenda salute* here has not been translated 'in caring for our salvation.'

[5] Cf. *De laps.* 16.

[6] Cf. Eph. 4.22; Col. 3.9.

[7] Matt. 19.17. 'attain to life': *ad vitam venire*; Vulg. *ad vitam ingredi.*

[8] John 15.14 f. Cyprian's punctuation differs from ours, and he has completed the sense by adding 'but friends,' either from the preceding sentence or from the next. 'what I command': *quod mando*; Vulg. *quae ego praecipio.* 'I call you': *dico vos*; Vulg. *dicam vos.* Cyprian repeats the quotation in the same form in *Ep.* 63.14.

[9] 'who so act': *denique.* As elsewhere in Cyprian (e.g. *Ad Donat.* 2; *De dom. orat.* 24; *Ep.* 11.7), *denique*, instead of signifying 'finally' (which is rare, Watson 316), takes on the meaning 'for this reason,' 'in consequence of this.' So here: 'because they keep the commandments.' Cf. LCP 6.84; Grasmüller 39.

[10] 'founded in massive security upon a rock': *super petram robusta mole fundatos*—an 'ablative of result,' cf. LCP 5.123 f.; 9.65 ff. Though Cyprian so frequently describes the Church as built *on Peter* and not 'upon a rock' (cf. ch. 4 with n. 31), he sees the faithful Christians as *fundati super petram* both here and in *Ep.* 37.4; 55.3; cf. *De hab. virg.* 2 (*solidati*) (Watson 280). Thus he distinguishes his use of Matt. 7.24 from that of Matt. 16.18; their connection seems to have been in his mind (this passage preparing for ch. 4), but he does not stress it.

[11] Matt. 7.24 f. *similabo eum*; Vulg. *assimilabitur.*—*advenerunt flumina, venerunt venti et inpegerunt*; Vulg. *et venerunt flumina et flaverunt venti et*

irruerunt.—fuit; Vulg. *erat.* The text of MS k is identical with that of Cyprian. The other O.L. readings differ from it and among themselves.

[12] *fidem* .·. . *servare mandati:* lit. 'keep the faith of the command.' *Fides* already meant belief, trust, faith etc., as between men, including the loyalty sworn to a superior. When the word was Christianized, besides loyalty to God (or Christ), it stood for *belief* (faith) in what He had said, and also for *what* was so believed. The one word for 'belief' and 'loyalty' made possible expressions which cannot be translated neatly; even a paraphrase will tend to say both too little and too much.

[13] 'who does not keep to the true way of salvation': *qui salutaris viae non tenet veritatem.* An artificial construction, the so-called *genetivus inversus,* in which a quality of something is underlined, the thing itself being made to depend on it in the genitive; for *veram (salutis) viam* (cf. LCP 5.86 f.; 9.17–19; cf. *De laps.* 30 n. 149, *De unit.* 14 n. 121). Here, the context and the final, emphatic, position of *veritatem* require that the 'true road' should refer back to 'what Christ commanded.'

[14] This and the next two sentences form only one in the original.

[15] 'deliverance': *sospitandis*; cf. Watson 196, 249, 310: an 'old ceremonial term of heathen worship,' used again by Cyprian for *salvare* in another rhetorical passage (*De hab. virg.* 2). The whole passage is reminiscent of Isa. 42.6 f. and 35.5 f.

[16] 'using the Christian name itself': *ut sub ipso christiani nominis titulo.* So too *De laps.* 15 (cf. n. 57): *sub misericordiae titulo. Sub* adds a touch of local imagery to an instrumental ablative; cf. our 'under the aegis of.' Other examples later in this same chapter: *sub obtentu spei, sub praetexto fidei, sub vocabulo Christi.* But there is no *sub* where it is purely instrumental—cf. *De laps.* 16: *quid inpietatem vocabulo pietatis adpellant?* (LCP 9.56 f.).

[17] 'to sunder our unity': *scinderet unitatem.* The first mention of the main subject. As was suggested above (Introd. n. 6a), the two meanings, 'uniqueness' and 'unity,' are regular in this treatise, one often sliding into the other, so that it is at times difficult to say which is intended. The same ambiguity is found even in modern documents, e.g. *Satis cognitum* (1896): Denzinger, *Enchir. Symb.* 1954 ff.

[18] This sentence really only ends at 'with trickery,' near the end of the chapter.

[19] This is a motif that kept recurring in the *De lapsis*: that those who went their own way, independently of the legitimate authorities, were sinning against the Gospel and the commands of Christ. The *De unitate* proceeds to prove it.

[20] Cf. 2 Cor. 11.14 f.

20a 'recklessness . . . hope': *desperationem sub obtentu spei*: cf. *De laps.* 22 (see n. 109). The recklessness, as we say, of desperation; cf. *Ep.* 59.14: *si paucis desperatis et perditis . . . videtur.*

21 'go back to the origin of [the Christian] realities, . . . their source': *ad veritatis originem . . . reditur . . . caput. Veritatis,* i.e. the permanent realities, not any abstract 'truth.' The same idea is implied in ch. 12: *veritatis caput adque originem reliquerunt,* and in *Ep.* 63.1: *veritatis luce perspecta, ad radicem adque originem traditionis dominicae revertatur.* What the 'origin and source' is, he explains in the next chapter.

22 'heavenly Master'; reading *magistri caelestis,* with many MSS, in place of *magisterii.*

23 'summed up in a matter of fact': *compendio veritatis.* It is not abstract 'truth' or teaching that is meant, but Christ's *action* with regard to Peter.

24 'to Peter': *ad Petrum.* The accepted use of *ad* after a verb of speaking (instead of the dative) was peculiar to Christian Latin, though no doubt common enough in popular language. Its entry into cultured circles came from the Bible, in the first place with indeclinable names (*dixit Dominus ad Noe,* Gen. 8.15 [*Vetus Latina*]), especially where there was ambiguity (*dixitque rursus Pharao ad Joseph,* Gen. 41.41). This, coupled with the popular use, led to *ad* being used in translating the N.T. even when the Greek itself had not πρός, but the dative. In the Vulgate N.T., St. Jerome kept *ad* where the Greek read πρός, and occasionally elsewhere; in the O.T. he used both constructions, but preferred *ad* where the dative would have been ambiguous. Cf. LCP 5.105–107; cf. below, ch. 8 with n. 70, ch. 12 with n. 104.

25 Matt. 16.18 f., quoted also in *Ep.* 33.1. *tibi dico*; Vulg. *dico tibi.*—*istam petram*; Vulg. *hanc petram.*—*inferorum*; Vulg. *inferi.*—*vincent,* Vulg. *praevalebunt adversus.*—*tibi*; Vulg. *et tibi.*—*quae . . . erunt ligata*; Vulg. *quodcumque . . . erit ligatum.*—*quaecumque . . . erunt soluta*; Vulg. *quodcumque . . . erit solutum.*

Whatever may have been Cyprian's mind as to the Bishop of Rome's position in the Church, he deduces from this 'Petrine' text the authority of the bishops, each in his own church (cf. *Ep.* 33.1). His first step, the 'matter of fact,' is that of seeing in Christ's action of founding the Church on one man, the establishment of something which was of its essence one and indivisible.—On the double edition of the following passage, cf. Introd, 6–8.

25a John 21.17. Quoted by the Roman clergy, *Ep.* 8.1; and referred to by Cyprian in *De hab. virg.* 10.

26 'a like power to all the Apostles': *apostolis omnibus parem* . .

potestatem. Cyprian nowhere uses the modern distinction between orders and jurisdiction, and to introduce it here would be to falsify his thought. His conception may in part be illustrated by the propagation of the strawberry plant, whose runners give birth to fresh strawberry plants, each as complete as itself. Cyprian maintains the persistence of the 'oneness' *in spite of* this, as also *in spite of* the fact that the Apostles were all shepherds equally (cf. below). He does so by saying that Christ's intention was revealed when He made the Church begin from *one* man, and when He indicated the *one* flock. The fact that he twice admits that the Apostles had equal powers, and is at pains to show that this does not detract from his argument, is evidence that he was attributing no special power to Peter over the others, still less to his successors in the See of Rome. Such expressions are in harmony with Cyprian's ecclesiology generally, but are inexplicable if this edition is ascribed to a pro-Papal corrector in this or any later century (as is done by J. Le Moyne, 'Saint Cyprien est-il bien l'auteur de la rédaction brève du "De Unitate" chapitre IV?' *Rev. bénédict.* 63 [1953] 105 f.).

[27] 'the source and hallmark of the [Church's] oneness': *unitatis originem adque rationem.* Cyprian sees the 'oneness' of the associated bishops (and so, that of the Church) as originating in Peter and perpetuated by their powers being all ultimately derived from him (i.e. through the various lines of bishops which start from the Apostles and, ultimately, from Peter). The legitimate appointment of a bishop in one of these lines of succession guarantees that he is in the one and only association which derives from Peter; such a bishop bears the 'hallmark of the [Church's] oneness.' Cyprian thinks of one thing at a time; he is here establishing the *condicio sine qua non* for a bishop in the Church. He is not concerned with bishops who might later break away from the unity by heresy or schism; he is thinking of Novatian in Rome, where Cornelius was bishop already, and of his own malcontents who were flouting the authority which he had himself derived (ultimately) from Peter. ('Hallmark' now seems a better translation for *ratio* than 'pattern,' suggested in the article referred to in the next note.)

[28] 'A primacy is given to Peter': *primatus Petro datur*; cf. M. Bévenot, the article under this title in JTS n.s. 5 (1954) 19–35. To translate *primatus* by 'the primacy' is to contradict the context which speaks of all the Apostles as being equal in power, equally shepherds. Elsewhere in Cyprian the word is used of Esau's primogeniture (*De bon. pat.* 19), and also of Peter's position compared with Paul's, but only by way of contrast to Paul's being a 'late-comer' to the Apostolic body (*novellus et posterus, Ep.* 71.3). Since superior power has just been excluded, it

can only mean some kind of 'seniority.' This latter word, then, would give Cyprian's meaning, but since *primatus* could also (perhaps did already then) mean 'the primacy' in the technical, Papal, sense, an attempt has been made to preserve the ambiguity. In Cyprian's mind 'a primacy' would refer to Peter's having been empowered first (as the starting point for the like gift to all the rest); to others (especially in Rome, no doubt) it could mean the gift of superiority— *the* primacy.

[29] 'this oneness of Peter': *hanc Petri unitatem*. 1) This is the only phrase in this edition of which the reading can be said to be doubtful. '*Hanc* et Pauli *unitatem*' can be dismissed at once, as in this edition there is no quotation from St. Paul, and the reading only occurs in the MSS which contain both the editions in succession. '*Hanc* ecclesiae (suae) *unitatem*' is the only serious rival, but can be explained as a borrowing from the other edition. What chiefly favours the reading '*Hanc* Petri *unitatem*' is its presence in all the MSS of the conflated text, where in spite of its superficial obscurity, it was not displaced by the simple adoption of '*ecclesiae*' for '*Petri*.' For the different readings in the various forms of ch. 4 in the MSS, cf. M. Bévenot, *St. Cyprian's 'De Unitate' chap. 4 in the Light of the Manuscripts* (Rome 1937): the skeleton texts at the end. 2) The 'oneness' of Peter, for all its strangeness of expression, represents in Cyprian's mind the fact that Christ initiated the Church not with the 'multiplicity' of the Apostles, but with Peter alone. Christ could have begun with all the Apostles at once, but the uniqueness of His Church would not have been so obvious. By His action Christ made the uniqueness of the Church a matter of faith. Hence to break away from the 'oneness' originating in Peter was to be untrue to the *faith*.

[30] 'the Chair of Peter': *cathedram Petri*. The whole context is against restricting the meaning to 'the see of Rome.' Cyprian's argument is based on the unicity of the *origin* (in Peter) of Church and authority alike. The one authority was perpetuated in the legitimate successions of the bishops, and to break with one's bishop was to break with the one, Christ-established, authority, that is, the 'Chair of Peter.' Thus his argument was pertinent not only for Rome, where Novatian had broken with Cornelius (whose 'chair' was Peter's in a double sense), but also nearer home, where Felicissimus and his faction were in revolt against himself. However, for those who recognized the true primacy of the see of Rome, Cyprian's words (taken out of their context) would naturally express the necessity of communion with Rome. It is not unreasonable to suppose (until proof of the contrary is forthcoming) that such an interpretation, put upon his

words at the time of the baptismal controversy, led Cyprian to revise this chapter for its final edition.

[31] 'on one man': *super unum*, i.e. on Peter. Cyprian describes the Church as 'built on Peter' no less than ten times (Watson lists the passages, 255 f., restoring one of these as against Hartel's reading, *super petram*, which Cyprian never uses of the Church). But see also above, ch. 2 n. 10.

Cyprian begins his revision by making explicit what was only implicit in the original: that it was on *one* man that Christ built His Church. This is at once underlined by means of the contrast provided by the equality of all the Apostles (which had, before, merely been stated, but is now given Scriptural backing). The two Scripture texts now balance one another, and Cyprian feels no need for the second Petrine text which he had used, especially as there was no balancing text available making the Apostles shepherds too. Consequently, all reference to the 'one flock' drops out. Also, since (as we suppose) '*cathedra Petri*' had led to misunderstanding, all reference to the one Chair is dropped and the argument confined to proving the one Church. Reinforced by the text from the Canticle of Canticles, the conclusion, omitting 'Peter' and 'Chair' alike, now makes a breach with the one *Church* what constitutes a betrayal of the faith, and opposition to the *Church* that which involves forfeiture of its membership. If the wording has changed, the fundamental thought is unaltered.

[32] John 20.21–23. 'if you forgive etc.': *si cuius remiseritis peccata, remittentur illi*; *si cuius tenueritis, tenebuntur*; Vulg. *quorum remiseritis peccata, remittuntur eis, et quorum retinueritis, retenta sunt*. Quoted again *Ep.* 69.11; 73.7; 75.16 (Firmilian).

[33] 'unique': *una*. 'United' is not the primary meaning here; and to translate 'one' would also imply that it is. Of course, 'unique' does not exclude 'united'; quite the contrary.

[34] Cant. 6.8. 'to her mother etc.': *una est matri suae, electa genetrici suae*; Vulg. *una est matris suae, electa genetrici suae*: 'she is the only one of her mother, the chosen of her that bore her' (Douay).—The symbol of the dove for the Church (see below, ch. 9) was especially popular with writers in N. Africa (e.g. Tertullian, Optatus): cf. F. J. Dölger, 'Unserer Taube Haus,' *Antike u. Christentum* 2 (1930) 47 f.

[35] 'Seeing that the blessed Apostle Paul. . . .' The rest of this edition (down to '. . . perversion of the truth') corresponds to nothing in the other edition. These 'last nine lines,' as they have been called (cf. M. Bévenot, *op. cit.* 44–51), constitute the strongest evidence that the edition which contains them was not the first. If it had been, the writer of the other had no reason for cutting them out, even if some editing

might have been necessary. But, on the opposite hypothesis, there was every reason for making some such insertion, when the revisor had only the shorter text before him. In the course of his revision, he had cut out all reference to the shepherds, and whereas the original text ended with the denunciation of a breach with one's bishop, he had now turned it into a breach with 'the Church.' Yet the next sentence dealt with the unity of the *bishops*! Following naturally as it did before, it now had to be led up to. Hence 'the last nine lines'—of not altogether irrelevant padding—were inserted to introduce the bishops, in view of: *Episcopatus unus est.* . . . (Substantially the same conclusion was reached simultaneously and independently by Dr. Othmar Perler— cf. 'Zur Datierung der beiden Fassungen des vierten Kapitels De Unitate Ecclesiae,' in *Röm. Quartalschrift* 44 [1936] 1–44; and 'De catholicae ecclesiae Unitate cap. 4–5. Die ursprünglichen Texte, ihre Überlieferung, ihre Datierung,' *ibid.* 151–68.)

36 'the mystery of Oneness': *sacramentum unitatis.* The word *sacramentum* here represents the word μυστήριον, as e.g. in Eph. 5.32 (cf. LCP 9.7).

37 Eph. 4.4–6. 'one hope of your calling': *una spes vocationis vestrae*; Vulg. *sicut vocati estis in una spe vocationis vestrae.* Quoted in whole or in part by two of the bishops in the Council of 256 (*Sent. Episc.* 1 and 5) —but in the Vulgate form.

38 'this oneness we must hold to etc.' This passage, which is most naturally understood as an appeal by Cyprian to his fellow bishops for unity among themselves, led most commentators to ascribe the treatise to the Council of 251. But the rest of the treatise is clearly addressed not to a Council of bishops but to his people as a whole, and the appeal here made is most easily explained as an insertion by Cyprian himself when he republished it later. Even if it might have been spoken in a general address, the passage would have implied a fear of discord among the bishops. But there were no grounds for such a fear when he first wrote the *De unitate*; Novatian had not yet (cf. *Ep.* 55.24) multiplied his 'pseudo-bishops' in opposition to the legitimate holders of the sees, and, even so, Cyprian never considered them as bishops at all. The fear of episcopal discord scarcely arose till the baptismal controversy, and Cyprian's sentiments here belong rather to that period which, for other reasons too, may be taken as the date of this revision. It is to be noted that the expression of his anxiety follows immediately upon a reference to *baptism*; (that is to say, in the quotation from St. Paul—a quotation which, with the two others introduced here, is characteristic of the baptismal controversy, and not found earlier in his writings. Cf. D. van den Eynde, 'La double édition du "De Unitate" de S. Cyprien,' *Rev. d'hist. ecclés.* 29 [1933] 5–24).

39 'bishops': *episcopi*. Equally common is *sacerdotes* (cf. *De laps.* 6 with n. 20), which stresses the sacred character of their office rather than its authority—which latter is to the fore here.

40 'to demonstrate.' Unity among the bishops in insisting on the 'oneness' of the Church (and of its baptism) will be a demonstration of their own Christ-given oneness. It will also show that they are 'undivided.'

41 'the true content of the faith': reading *fidei veritatem* with all the MSS except S (which Hartel follows). Another instance of the *genetivus inversus* (cf. above, n. 13); it equals *veram fidem*. Its 'true content' is 'the oneness of the Church'; cf. above, n. 29 (2).

42 'The authority of the bishops forms a unity': *Episcopatus unus est*. *Episcopatus* is not used by Cyprian in the sense of the body of the bishops (*corpus* or *collegium*), and the preceding context excludes the translation 'the bishop's local authority.' It must stand for the episcopal authority throughout the Church, all derived from Peter (cf. Bévenot, '*Primatus Petro datur*,' JTS n.s.5 [1954] 28).

43 'his part,' i.e. the authority in his own church, or, as we should say, 'in his own diocese.'—'in its totality': *in solidum*, a legal phrase implying indivisibility in the object concerned (cf. M. Bévenot, '"*In solidum*" and St. Cyprian,' in JTS n.s.6 [1955] 244–48). He uses it paradoxically here, since, in the mind of the jurists, a number of 'parts' each held *in solidum* would no longer constitute an *unum*. But the unity of the bishops among themselves is something transcending the juridical sphere, being secured, according to Cyprian, by the 'cement of concord': *concordiae mutuae glutino* (*Ep.* 68.3; cf. *Ep.* 66.8 and, below—of the Church in general—ch. 23 with n. 188a). As for the 'indivisibility' of diocesan authority (i.e. its being held *in solidum*), Cyprian often spoke of the 'independence' of each local bishop, though even for him it was not the whole of the matter (cf. article referred to in Introd. n. 12). It was particularly in place here, in view of the challenge to episcopal authority at the time, both in Carthage and in Rome (cf. below, ch. 8 and n. 66).

44 *exundantis copiae largitate*, cf. *De laps.* 21 n. 106. So too below: 'in generous growth': *copia ubertatis*.

45 *unitas servatur in origine*. Some might be tempted to see in this a clue which would lead to quite a different interpretation of these two chapters—that here Cyprian recognizes the need of an abiding *contemporary* source (*origo*). With that supposition would agree the fact that the bishop of Rome holds the *locus Petri* (*Ep.* 55.8), and that in

Rome is the *cathedra Petri et ecclesia principalis unde unitas sacerdotalis exorta est* (*Ep.* 59.14). The conclusion would then follow that Cyprian was indeed speaking of the see of Rome, when he asked whether deserting the *Chair of Peter* did not mean being outside the Church. (This position is ably presented by Abbot B. C. Butler: 'St. Cyprian on the Church' I, *Downside Rev.* 71 [1952–3] 1–13; II, *ibid.* 258–72; see especially 265 ff.)

But, apart from anything else, the structure of Cyprian's thought seems against it. That same structure is found again in *Ep.* 74.10 which is full of reminiscences of *De unit.* chs. 3, 5, and 6. The ridding oneself of error, he says, can be 'summed up' as a return to the 'source and origin.' If the water in a stream dries up, you inspect its course to see what has blocked the flow of water from its 'source.' So now, when some sort of deficiency about the truth has shown itself, the bishops must return to the Christ-given source, as preserved in the Gospel and the apostolic tradition (i.e. St. Paul), and see that their action bears the stamp of that origin (*ut . . . inde surgat actus nostri ratio unde et ordo et origo surrexit*). The 'source,' the 'origin' in question can only be Christ's own action and not some contemporary norm; for in the most vehement of all his letters against Pope Stephen, Cyprian can hardly be supposed to be stressing the need of conformity with Rome.

No doubt, in our present passage, when he speaks of the *one* mother, of whose womb we are born, etc., he is speaking of something contemporary. But that is the Church itself, which exists now by remaining continuous with its source in the past, not (in his view) by contact with such a source in the present (cf. Introd. n. 13).

[46] *avelle radium . . . divisionem lucis unitas non capit.* An example of a graphic present with future meaning; cf. *De laps.* 20 n. 100.

[47] 'the spouse of Christ'; cf. 2 Cor. 11.2 and especially Eph. 5.23–32, which are respectively commented on in *Ep.* 75.14 (Firmilian), and in 52.1 and 69.2. These commentaries all take up ideas broached here. —The adultery motif applies (as here) to schismatics when they leave the Church to attach themselves to another body ('enters on an adulterous union'); and to 'heretics' when they attempt to 'corrupt' the Church (cf. Susanna and the elders, as in *Ep.* 43.4).

[47a] *regno adsignat*—by Confirmation.

[48] An idea taken up again in *Ep.* 74.7. Cf. also ch. 23 n. 183.

[49] In *Ep.* 69.2 and 74.11 Cyprian develops the idea of Noe's ark on the basis of 1 Pet. 3.20 f.

[50] [No] 'escape for one who is found to be outside the Church': *qui extra ecclesiam foris fuerit* [*non*] *evadit.* Cyprian's rigidity in applying the dogma of the necessity of the Church is well known (cf. *Ep.* 73.21:

salus extra ecclesiam non est, and below, 14: *occidi talis potest, coronari non potest*, etc.). It is the basis of his stand against heretical baptism. His mistakes are more excusable than those of his later imitators who have the teaching of so many more centuries of the Church's experience to guide them.

The unavoidability of the result is underlined by the use of the present tense *evadit*, even after *foris fuerit*. This use of the present for the future became very common in Christian literature, since matters of faith, even regarding the future, are so real to the Christian that they can be visualized as already present; so below, ch. 14 (n. 111), *De laps.* 20 (n. 100) (cf. LCP 9.73–79, where many instances are given from Cyprian's treatises).

51 Matt. 12.30, quoted again in *Test.* 3.86, with *mecum colligit* inverted. MS k agrees with the text here. *adversus me*; other O.L. and Vulg., *contra me.—mecum colligit*; other O.L. and Vulg., *congregat mecum.—spargit*; so too Vulg.; but O.L. (including k, second hand), *dispargit*.

52 John 10.30.

53 1 John 5.8. One might be forgiven for thinking that Cyprian read the famous 'Johannine comma' (v. 7) in his text. In fact, he was only giving an allegorical interpretation of 'the spirit and the water and the blood' in terms of the Trinity, as did several of the Latin Fathers after him (including St. Augustine), though they certainly did not read the interpolation. However, it is likely enough that the subsequent creation of verse 7 (in Spain, middle of the 4th century) was prompted by Cyprian's words here. On the whole question, see T. Ayuso's articles in *Biblica* 28 and 29 [Rome 1947–48] 'Nuevo estudio sobre el "Comma Joanneum,"' especially 29.53 f., 70; and, for more detail on Cyprian, A. Bludau: 'Das "Comma Johanneum" bei Tertullian und Cyprian,' *Theol. Quartalschr.* 101 (1920) 1–28.

54 'from the stability of God': *de divina firmitate*; cf. Watson 244.

55 'after the celestial pattern': *sacramentis caelestibus*, i.e. the oneness in the Trinity. Poukens (in de Ghellinck 199 f.) translates: 'resting on divine precepts.' But the examples which he quotes do not bear him out, and though it is true that there is only one God, yet the three Persons provide a basis for the plural here. The thought is developed in the following chapter (e.g. '"from the upper parts," that is, from His Father in heaven').—In *Ep.* 74.10 (which has several reminiscences of *De unit.*), *sacramentorum caelestium* (*ratione*) would seem to mean 'the heavenly truths of our Faith'

[56] On unity within the Church as being based on the Trinity, cf. *De dom. orat.* 23 (*fin.*) and 30.

[57] 'This holy mystery of oneness': *hoc unitatis sacramentum.*

[58] 'when they draw lots': *sortientibus.* An ablative absolute, without the subject being expressed. It is not a dative of the agent, since the coat is won not by the *sortientes,* but only by one of them. See LCP 9.34 f.

[59] John 19.23 f.: *de tunica autem quia de superiore parte non consutilis sed per totum textilis fuerat*; Vulg. *erat autem tunica inconsutilis desuper contexta per totum.* Cyprian's seems to be a free rendering, especially in the order of the words; other O.L. texts differ from it and among themselves.—'from the upper part.' This phrase, coming first in Cyprian's text, need not mean the top of the coat, but could be taken as he takes it in the next sentence.

[60] 'with which He was clothed': *unitatem ille portabat.* The mystical pregnancy of Cyprian's thought defies translation. *Portare* is used of what Christ *assumed* in the Incarnation, primarily His sacred humanity (e.g. in the agony He showed *infirmitatem hominis quem portabat*—see *De dom. orat.* 14; cf. *Tu, ad liberandum suscepturus hominem* in the *Te Deum*); but the idea of the Mystical Body is never far away (*in uno omnes ipse portavit*—ibid. 8), and is linked with the Redemption: *nos omnes portabat Christus qui et peccata nostra portabat* (*Ep.* 63.13; cf. *De bono pat.* 6). The 'oneness' or unity which He brought from heaven and bestowed on those who have 'put on Christ' (cf. below), is illustrated by the Eucharist, where, by means of the bread which is made by the union of many grains of corn, Christ *populum nostrum, quem portabat, indicat adunatum* (*Ep.* 69.5; cf. Watson 248 and 249).

[61] 'For this reason, by contrast': *contra denique.* For this meaning of *denique,* cf. above, ch. 2 n. 9.

[62] 3 Kings 11.31 f., 36. 'ten sceptres': *decem sceptra,* a reading reproducing a mistranslation of the original by the LXX, the same Heb. word meaning both 'tribe' and 'wand'; Vulg. *decem tribus.*—'two sceptres': *duo sceptra.* So too the LXX; probably a correction, as 'one tribe,' the Heb. (and Vulg.) reading, has the appearance of being a slip. However 'the prophet is not concerned with arithmetic'—K. Smyth, *Cath. Commentary on Holy Scripture* (London 1953) 270e.

[63] 'sacred symbolism': *sacramento et signo,* hendiadys; and cf. *Ep.* 63.12 *sacramentum rei illius,* i.e. the *significance* of the water turned to wine at Cana.

[64] 'was proclaimed': *declaravit.* The subject of the Latin verb seems to be *scriptura divina,* which introduced the quotation from St. John, above.

⁶⁵ John 10.16. *Unus grex* follows the Greek. Vulg. has *unum ovile*, 'one fold' (Douay).—Quoted again *Ep.* 69.5.

⁶⁶ This seems to be a clear reference to Novatian and the schism inaugurated by him in Rome. The schism of Felicissimus had not yet created a second 'shepherd' in opposition to Cyprian; Fortunatus was only made 'bishop' there later (cf. *Ep.* 59.9–11).—On the other hand, it does not justify the contention that the whole treatise has only the unity of each local church in view. Chapter 5 alone is sufficient to disprove this (cf. B. C. Butler, *art. cit., Downside Rev.* [1952–3] 265 ff.). In fact, it is the oneness of the universal Church that makes the idea of a split in a local church intolerable. Needless to say, Cyprian did not envisage the possibility of coadjutor bishops, or of bishops of different Rites in the same place. However, these are not set up in opposition to one another, which is what he excludes here.

⁶⁷ I Cor. 1.10. 'knit together': *compositi* (κατηρτισμένοι); Vulg. *perfecti*: 'perfect' (Douay).—'judgment': *sententia*; so too Vulg., but most O.L. texts read *scientia*. Also quoted in *Test.* 3.86.

⁶⁸ Eph. 4.2 f. 'striving': *satis agentes*, (σπουδάζοντες); Vulg. *solliciti*: 'careful' (Douay). Quoted again *De bon. pat.* 15, and *Ep.* 55.24.

⁶⁹ 'hold his own or survive': *stare et vivere*. Both words in a spiritual sense: the *stantes* were the faithful, generally in contrast with the *lapsi*; *vivere* suggests *in Christo*.

⁷⁰ 'it was said to Rahab': *dictum sit ad Rhaab*. For *ad* in place of the dative, cf. ch. 4 n. 24.—It is difficult to tell how Cyprian spelt the name Rahab. On Rahab, and on the Pasch (below), cf. *Ep.* 69.4.

⁷¹ Jos. 2.18 f.; also quoted in *Ep.* 69.4. 'his blood shall be on his own head': *reus sibi erit*, which represents the LXX literally. This is best translated 'his blood etc.,' which, however, is precisely what the Heb. and Vulg. say—an instance of a Hebrew idiom which has become completely acclimatized in English.

⁷² 'the sacred meaning of the Pasch': *sacramentum Paschae*. *Sacramentum*, here, is a type or figure having an inner meaning which came to be recognized in its 'fulfilment' in the New Testament. The Pasch was a figure of the Passion and of the Eucharist, and Cyprian sees in 'the one house' where the lamb should be eaten (Exod. 12.46), a type whose inner meaning was fulfilled in the one Church in which alone the Eucharist might be celebrated.

⁷³ Exod. 12.46. 'cast outside': *eicietis*. The Latin word is characteristic of the so-called 'African' O.L. (cf. A. V. Billen, *The Old Latin Texts of the Heptateuch* [Cambridge 1927] 24); Vulg. *efferetis*: 'carry forth' (Douay). Quoted in *Test.* 3.86; also in *Ep.* 69.4, where the text is used to show that 'the Church is not to be found outside, and cannot be

split in two or divided (*nec scindi adversum se aut dividi posse*), but that it maintains the unity and wholeness of an indivisible house.'

74 Ps. 67 [Heb. 68].7. 'who are of one mind': *unanimes*; Vulg. *unius moris*: 'men of one manner' (Douay). Watson (305) gives good grounds for suspecting that Cyprian used the form *unianimes*. The new Psalter: *derelictis*, 'God prepareth a home for the abandoned (neglected).' Cyprian's reading enabled him to quote it (as he often did) when appealing for peace and unity.

75 'a dove': *columba*. The taste for allegory was given much scope by the dove, owing to its Scriptural appearances after the flood, in the Canticle of Canticles, and at Our Lord's baptism. Its specific characteristics, real or mythical, received a spiritual interpretation which in many cases became traditional throughout the Middle Ages. Here Cyprian must have been using some current list which it would be difficult to trace. Tertullian speaks of the dove's 'simplicity,' i.e. its harmlessness and its faithfulness to its mate (which latter is untrue) —cf. *De Monog.* 8, and *ad loc.* W. P. Le Saint, ACW 13. 161 n. 115; also of its literally having no gall—*De bapt.* 8. This idea, which is also false (as might have been seen from Pliny, *Nat. hist.* 11.194), is perhaps first found in Clement of Alexandria (*Paed.* 1.5.14). As for 'hatching their young together,' Aristotle tells us that the cock sits on the eggs by day and the hen at night, and that they similarly share the task of keeping the nurslings warm (*Hist. an.* 562b.; cf. Pliny, *Nat. hist.* 10.159). Their 'keeping formation' when in flight was said to keep the hawk away by the noise of their wings. Some of these points are found in the *Physiologus*, a descriptive catalogue of animals, metals, etc., to each of which a Christian symbolical meaning was attached. This may already have been in existence in some form at our period, but cannot explain Cyprian's list as a whole. (For 'Physiologus' cf. PG 43.526B [on the dove] and better texts in F. Sbordone's edition [Milan 1936].) On the whole question, cf. RE IV A II (1932), *s.v.* 'Taube.'

76 'it loves. . . .' This and all the following verbs are in the infinitive.

77 'hatch,' reading *edere* with Hartel. The alternative reading *alere* gives easier sense, but has little MS support and looks like a well-meaning correction.

78 'love for our brethren': *dilectio fraternitatis*. It might also be construed as a subjective genitive—'the love which the brethren practise.'

79 'harbour': lit. 'What is the fierceness etc. . . . doing in a Christian's breast?'

80 'break away from the Church': *de ecclesia separantur*. An instance of the *ablativus separativus* being replaced by a prepositional phrase.

Cyprian uses *de ecclesia perire* several times in his letters, and *ab ecclesia perire* once. He also uses *de* with *liberare*, *excludere*, and *purgare*, but with the last and with *separare* also *ab*. See LCP 5.109 f. and 9.44 f.

81 'on these men fall the curse and the rod': *hos execratur et percutit.*

82 1 John 2.19. 'went out': *exierunt*; Vulg. *prodierunt*;—'were not': *non fuerunt*; Vulg. *non erant*;—'For if': *Si enim*; Vulg. *Nam si*;—'they would have stayed': *mansissent*; Vulg. *permansissent utique.* Quoted also in *Test.* 3.78; *Ep.* 59.7; 69.1; 70.3.

83 'disloyal trouble-makers': *perfidia discordans.*

84 'leaving man's freedom unimpaired': *manente propriae libertatis arbitrio.* Cf. *Ep.* 59.7: by His question, 'Will you also go away?' (John 6.68), Christ Himself respects the rule *qua homo libertati suae relictus et in arbitrio proprio constitutus, sibimet ipse vel mortem adpetit vel salutem.*

85 1 Cor. 11.19. 'those approved': *probati*; Vulg. *et qui probati sunt.* —'may be': *sint*; Vulg. *fiant.* Quoted also in *Test.* 3.93.

86 Cf. Matt. 3.12. Whereas here he uses the text to illustrate the distinction of the just and unjust 'even before the day of judgment,' later he uses it (with the parable of the cockle) to exclude the discriminations which Novatian made before 'the day of the Lord' (*Ep.* 54.3, 55.25; cf. Bévenot, 'St. Cyprian and the Papacy,' *Dublin Rev.* 228 [1954] 167; and 'Penance and the *De lapsis*,' *Theol. Stud.* 16 [1955] 191).

86a 'certain people . . . seize authority': *sunt qui (=quidam) se . . . praeficiunt.* Indicative mood for subjunctive in relative clauses of an undefined antecedent—cf. A. Blaise, *Manuel de latin chrétien* (Strasbourg 1955) §319.

87 'appointment': *ordinationis.* Thornton in *Library of the Fathers* translates: 'without any lawful rite of ordination' (similarly other translators). But the modern word 'ordination' has associations which were certainly then absent from the ordinary use of the Latin word; cf. below, ch. 17 with n. 140 and ch. 18 with n. 145, which passages of themselves show that the useful treatment of the word in LCP 8.51, needs supplementing. Cf. Blaise-Chirat, *s.v.* 5.

87a This sentence seems to be another clear reference to Novatian's schism. Cf. *Ep.* 69.5 (a letter with many reminiscences of the *De unitate*): *manente vero pastore et in ecclesia Dei ordinatione succedanea praesidente, nemini succedens et a se ipse incipiens* [Novatianus], *alienus fit* etc.

88 Cf. Ps. 1.1.

89 'canker': so too in *De laps.* 34 (n. 165). Cf. 2 Tim. 2.17, quoted in *Test.* 3.78; and *Ep.* 59.20.

90 'preaching': *tractatus*. Thornton translates 'writings'; but cf. G. Bardy, '*Tractare, tractatus*,' in *Rech. de sc. rel.* 33 (1946) 211–35, showing that Cyprian introduced the technical meaning of 'the sermon' into these words. Hence what are commonly known as Cyprian's 'treatises' are almost all public addresses ; cf. the preface to his *Testimonia*, which are collections of Scripture texts grouped under many headings: his object, he says, was *non tam tractasse quam tractantibus materiam praebuisse*; see Watson 271 f.

91 Jer. 23.16 f. 'the word of the Lord': *verbum Domini*.—'to him who': *omni*. The readings *Domini* and *omni* represent the LXX κυρίου and παντί, and have here been preferred to Hartel's *Dei* and *omnis*. The first correction is also supported by *Ep.* 43.5; the latter by *te* at the end of the passage.

92 Jer. 23.21 f. 'support': *substantia* from ὑπόστασις in the LXX; Vulg. *consilio*: 'counsel' (Douay).—'had they taught them': *et si docuissent*, words missing in the LXX as we have it.—'thoughts': *cogitationibus* (so too Vulg.); LXX ἐπιτηδευμάτων (pursuits, practices). Found also elsewhere with this sense: cf. Rönsch 308.

93 Jer. 2.13. 'the fountain of the water of life': *fontem aquae vitae*. An alternative reading is *vivae*; both have the authority of different LXX MSS.—'cannot': *non possunt*, here and in *Ep.* 70.1. But *Test.* 1.3 gives *non poterunt* which agrees with LXX; Vulg. *non valent*.

94 'the one baptism etc.' For Cyprian, it went without saying that outside the Church there was no valid baptism at all. The strength of his conviction led to the famous baptismal controversy later. Though Pope Stephen maintained the traditional attitude of the Church against him, it took time before this was recognized without question universally.

95 'but only': *sed immo*. Equivalent to *sed potius* in the preceding phrase. Cyprian availed himself of the alternative for the rhythmical endings (Grasmüller 40 f.; De Jonge, *op. cit.* 41).

96 'peace': *pacis*. Cyprian plays on the literal meaning of the technical word for reconciliation or communion with the Church.

97 'certain people': *quidam*. Cyprian's audience would recognize whom he meant. Obviously the text had been used to justify independent action.

98 Matt. 18.20; cf. next note.

99 Matt. 18.19 f. 'that if etc.': *quoniam si duobus . . . convenerit in terra . . . quamcumque petieritis, continget vobis*; Vulg. *quia si duo . . . consenserint super terram . . . quamcumque petierint, fiet illis.*—*Ubicumque enim fuerint duo aut tres collecti . . . ego cum eis sum*; Vulg. *Ubi enim sunt* *duo vel tres congregati . . . ibi sum in medio eorum.*—Quoted again in *Test.* 3.3 and *Ep.* 11.3 (v. 19 only). MS e has Cyprian's readings.

[100] *fideliter et firmiter.* Hartel puts this with *docuit*, but it goes more naturally with *conveniat nobis.*

[101] 'it is not we etc.' The same idea was poignantly expressed by Cyprian in his letter to the Roman confessors when they were still supporting Novatian (*Ep.* 46.2): *quia nos ecclesia derelicta foras exire et ad vos venire non possumus. . . .*

[102] 'in opposition': *diversa*, in the sense of 'hostile' (Watson 294).

[103] 'the source and origin itself of [the Christian] realities': *veritatis caput adque originem*; cf. ch. 3 (end) for the wording, and ch. 4 for the thought. A new schism, breaking with the episcopal successions already in existence, loses contact with the 'source and origin.'

[104] *ad hos . . . loquitur. Ad* in place of a dative after a verb of speaking; cf. ch. 4 n. 24.

[104a] 'shall': *possint*—cf. ch. 20 n. 165. Here, a helpful substitute for a future subjunctive.

[105] Cf. Dan. 3.49–51, and *De laps.* 31.

[106] Cf. Acts 16.25 f. The two Apostles were Paul and Silas.

[107] Mark 11.25. *Et cum steteritis ad orationem, remittite . . . remittat peccata vobis*; Vulg. *Et cum stabitis ad orandum, dimittite . . . dimittat vobis peccata vestra.* Quoted also in *Test.* 3.22 and *De dom. orat.* 23.

[108] Cf. Matt. 5.23 f., quoted in *Test.* 3.3.

[109] Cf. Gen. 4.5, and *De dom. orat.* 24.

[110] 'opponents of the priests': *aemuli sacerdotum*, i.e. 'hostile to'— cf. Watson 295; Rönsch 338.

[111] 'the guilt . . . removed': *macula ista . . . abluitur.* Another case of the present tense in place of the future, expected after *si . . . fuerit.* The slaying is future; the irremovability of their guilt is seen as present, absolute. Cf. ch. 6 with n. 50, and *De laps.* 20 with n. 100.

[112] 'schism': *discordia*—the actual reality being expressed by the abstract term (Watson 294). So too *passio.* Cf. *De laps.* 4 and n. 17.— 'irremissible': *inexpiabilis*, i.e. so long as it is persisted in.

[113] 'kingdom . . . to be its queen': *ad regnum . . . regnatura est.* The Latin underlines the identity of the Church here with the Church finally triumphant in heaven.

[114] I Cor. 13.2–5, 7 f. Also quoted (with v. 6) in *Test.* 3.3; but both omit 'is not ambitious, seeketh not her own' in v. 5. Here Cyprian seems to be quoting from memory, as he puts 'dealeth not perversely' out of place. In *Test.* 3.3 for *caritas*, some of the best MSS read *agape* throughout, which may well have been the original reading of the O.L. (Watson 297; von Soden 67–69). Apart from this, he always

uses *caritas* or *dilectio* (cf. Pétré, *op. cit.* 45 ff.), but it is worthy of notice that he uses *agape* in the title of that chapter (both there and in his table at the beginning of *Test.* 3).

'should have faith': Cyprian omits *omnem*.—'have not' (twice): *non habeam*; Vulg. *non habuero*.—'distribute all my goods': *in cibos distribuero omnia mea*; Vulg. *distribuero in cibos omnes facultates meas*:— 'to be burned': *ut ardeam*; Vulg. *ita ut ardeam*.—'I profit nothing': *nihil proficio*; Vulg. *nihil mihi prodest*.—'great-hearted': *magnanima*; Vulg. *patiens* (μακροθυμεῖ).—'loveth all things': *omnia diligit* (perhaps from a reading στέργει); Vulg. *omnia suffert* (στέγει).—'shall never fall away': *numquam excidet*; Vulg. *numquam excidit*.

[115] John 15.12. 'commandment': *mandatum*; Vulg. *praeceptum*.— 'as': *quemadmodum*; Vulg. *sicut*. The same text in *Test.* 3.3.

[116] 'Christ . . . cannot reward him': *ad praemium Christi . . . pertinere non poterit*.

[117] 1 John 4.16. 'love': *dilectio*; Vulg. *caritas*.—'he that abideth in God, abideth in love': *qui manet in Deo in dilectione manet* (so the great preponderance of MSS, besides those quoted by Hartel); Vulg. *qui manet in dilectione in Deo manet*.—'abideth in him': *in illo manet*; Vulg. *in eo*.

Quoted also in *Test.* 3.3, but without the inversion *in Deo, in dilectione*. Hence the inversion here may have been deliberate, as being dialectically more satisfying for his argument, and not contrary to John's mind (cf. von Soden, *op. cit.* 16, who quotes other instances in Cyprian of deliberate verbal alterations of Scripture texts).

[118] 'recklessness': *desperationis*; cf. *De unit.* ch. 3 n. 20a.—This is Cyprian's own deduction from 1 Cor. 13.3b quoted above; cf. ch. 19 and *Ep.* 73.21. A schism was, to him, a deliberate breach of charity. Lacking in charity, the schismatic could 'profit nothing.'

[119] Matt. 24.5. 'deceive': *fallent* (so, generally, in the O.L.; cf. Matzkow *in loc.*); Vulg. *seducent*. Quoted again *Ep.* 73.16 and 75.9 (Firmilian).—Hartel assigns this text erroneously to Mark 13.6.

[120] 'cannot be taken for': *nec . . . videri potest*. Perhaps, more simply, 'is not' (Watson 240, who gives several examples of *videri* used superfluously).

[121] 'the true faith': *(in) fidei veritate*; cf. above, ch. 2 n. 13.

[122] Matt. 7.22 f. (cf. *Test.* 3.26). 'turned out': *exclusimus*; Vulg. *eiecimus*. The latter is not used for 'casting out' (devils etc.) in the 'African' version, which has *excludere* or *expellere* instead of *eicere* (von Soden 325, 282).—'I never knew you. Begone': *numquam vos cognovi: recedite* (a characteristic 'African' reading, which should be restored at *Test.* 3.26); Vulg. *numquam novi vos, discedite*. Compounds with

re- were preferred to those with *dis-* (von Soden 283, 78 f.). Cf. Matzkow *in loc.*

[123] 'justice of life': *iustitia* (cf. Blaise-Chirat, *s.v.* 4).

[124] 'to conciliate God': *promereri Deum*; more generally 'to deserve well of, to render favourable': 'used by Cyprian at least thirty-three times. . . . The word did not hold its own in later theological literature' (Watson 280). Cf. below, ch. 18 n. 148, and *De laps.* 31 n. 154.

[125] Mark 12.29–31 (cf. Deut. 6.4 f.; and Matt. 22.37–39, which omits 'and with thy whole strength'). 'one Lord': *dominus unus* (LXX—Deut. 6.4: κύριος εἷς); Vulg. *Deus unus* (but *Dominus unus* in Deut. 6.4).—'with': *de* (throughout); Vulg. *ex* (throughout).— 'soul'; Cyprian omits *et ex tota mente tua* both here and *De dom. orat.* 28 and *Ad Fort.* 2.—'This comes first': *Hoc primum*; Vulg. *Hoc est primum mandatum.*—'and the second is like to it': *et secundum simile huic*; Vulg. *secundum autem simile est illi.*—'thyself': *te*; Vulg. *teipsum.* 'Thy neighbour': *proximum tuum*, as in the Vulg. But there is much evidence that in the O.L. Bible *proximum tibi* was the reading, and in several other Cyprianic passages *tibi* is found in many if not all of the good MSS (cf. von Soden 63, 73, 98 n.). In classical Latin, only the plural was used as a substantive; hence it was natural that at first the singular should be adjectival and so require *tibi*; (on the Christian use of *proximus* in general, cf. Pétré, *op. cit.* 135 and 141–60). The Vulg. reading of such a constantly repeated text would tend to oust the unfamiliar *tibi* from the MSS. Its presence at all in so many, suggests that it was original. In the present passage, it is found in at least two 9th-century MSS, one now in Leyden, the other in Oxford.

[126] Matt. 22.40. 'commandments': *praeceptis*; Vulg. *mandatis.*—'the whole law': *tota lex*; Vulg. *universa lex.*—The same combination of Mark 12.29–31 with this verse is found in *De dom. orat.* 28 and *Ad Fort.* 2.

[127] 'desecrates the Sacrament': *sacramentum profanat.* For once, *sacramentum* here, almost certainly, stands for the Eucharist—cf. above, ch. 13, and below, ch. 17: (the schismatic is) 'an enemy of the altar, a rebel against the sacrifice of Christ' (Poukens, in de Ghellinck 212).

[128] 2 Tim. 3.1–9. There are several interesting divergences from Vulg., of which the following are a selection. 'troublous': *molesta*; Vulg. *periculosa.*—'self-centred': *sibi placentes*; Vulg. *seipsos amantes.* —'heedless of their parents' word': *parentibus in dicto non audientes* (*non* should probably be omitted; cf. Hartel's apparatus here and at *Test.* 2.27; also Blaise-Chirat, *s.v.* 'indictoaudiens') ; Vulg. *parentibus non obedientes* (von Soden 151, 337).—'covenant-breakers': *sine foedere*; Vulg. *sine pace.*—'informers': *delatores*; Vulg. *criminatores.*—'not

lovers of the good': *bonum non amantes*; Vulg. *sine benignitate.*—'puffed up with conceit': *stupore inflati*; Vulg. *tumidi.*—'presenting a façade of piety': *habentes deformationem religionis*; Vulg. *habentes quidem speciem pietatis.*—'ravish': *praedari*; Vulg. *captivas ducunt* (αἰχμαλωτίζοντες). —'Moses': *Moysi* (according to Hartel); but C. H. Turner, after weighing the evidence, tentatively adopts the view that Cyprian always omitted the 'γ' ('Prolegomena to the *Testimonia* of St. Cyprian II,' in JTS 9 [1908] 80–82).—'they shall not proceed any further': *non proficient plurimum* (superlative used in a comparative sense [ἐπὶ πλεῖον]; cf. Rönsch 417 f.); Vulg. *ultra non proficient.*— 'ineptitude': *imperitia*; Vulg. *insipientia.*

¹²⁹ This passage is reminiscent of the end of *Ad Donat.* 3, where there occurs a similar succession of nouns and verbs, paired together.

¹³⁰ 'against them': *ab eiusmodi*, for *a talibus*, 'against such.' So too below, 'men of that stamp,' and the first words of ch. 11, *Contra eiusmodi*. But this use is not frequent (Watson 306).

¹³¹ Mark 13.23. 'But do you take heed': *Vos autem cavete*; Vulg. *Vos ergo videte.*—Clearly, prophecy in no way interferes with free will.

¹³² Ecclus. 28.28 (RV 24). The text agrees substantially with Vulg., since St. Jerome left the O.L. unchanged. Its considerable differences from LXX and from the Syriac Peshitta are explicable by the variety of the recensions of this book in the Hebrew itself, and by the subsequent combinations which were made in the successive versions. A comparison with the Revised Version will show this at a glance.— Cyprian quotes this verse identically also in *Test.* 3.95; *Ep.* 59.20; 66.7.

¹³³ 1 Cor. 15.33. *Conrumpunt ingenia bona confabulationes pessimae* (so too *Ep.* 59.20, and the better MSS of *Test.* 3.95); Vulg. *Corrumpunt mores bonos colloquia mala.*

¹³⁴ Matt. 15.14. *caecus autem caecum ducens*; MS e has *si caecum ducat* (cf. Augustine, *C. Faust.* 16.31); other O.L. MSS and Vulg. *si caeco ducatum dederit* (or *praestet*, etc.). Cyprian has *simul* with e against *ambo* (generally); but *cadent* (against e and Vulg.: *cadunt*) with several other O.L. MSS (Matzkow).—Also quoted in *Ep.* 43.5.

¹³⁵ This shows not only the necessity of belonging to the Church, but the possibility of exclusion without any positive act on the part of the Church such as formal excommunication.

¹³⁶ *pro fide perfidus*; cf. *De laps.* 22 n. 109.

¹³⁷ Membership of the Church was manifested by access to the Eucharist everywhere. Revolt from the Church was most manifest when independent eucharistic centres were set up. Cf. L. Hertling, 'Communio und Primat,' *Misc. hist. pont.* 7.10.

¹³⁸ 'a rival liturgy': *precem alteram. Prex* certainly stood for the

'Canon' of the Mass from St. Augustine's time, and though Cyprian uses *oratio* for it in one place (*De dom. orat.* 31), he may also have used *prex* (cf. J. A. Jungmann, *Missarum sollemnia* 2.2.2 ch. 1 nn. 4, 5, quoting Fortescue, but apparently with reservations).

[139] 'the reality of the divine Victim': *dominicae hostiae veritatem.*—*Dominicus* (for *Domini*) is an adjectival form equivalent to a genitive. The use is very frequent for a restricted number of Christian words (e.g. *divinus, ecclesiasticus, evangelicus, saecularis, caelestis*), usually in stereotyped combinations. It will have come from the official language of the Church, just as a similar use came from the language of the Roman Court, e.g. *cursor dominicus*, an Imperial messenger. Other cases of such non-Christian adjectival forms are of an artificial, rhetorical nature. Cf. below, ch. 22 and n. 180 (LCP 5.89–99; 9.23–30).

[140] 'institution': *ordinationem*; cf. ch. 10 and n. 87, and below, n. 145.

[141] *ob temeritatis audaciam*; cf. *De laps.* 21 and n. 106.

[142] Cf. Num. 16.1–33.

[143] Cf. Num. 16.35.

[144] *admonens scilicet*; i.e. 'naturally, of course, etc.' (Grasmüller 44).

[145] 'appointment': *ordinatio*; cf. ch. 10 and n. 87, ch. 17 and n. 140.

[146] Cyprian often uses this example of divine retribution in his letters; cf. *Ep.* 3.1, 67.3, 69.8 f., 73.8.

[147] Cf. 2 Par. 26.16–21.

[148] 'win the Lord's favour': *Dominum promerentur*; cf. ch. 15 n. 124.

[149] 'sealed'; a reference to the post-baptismal unction (cf. Augustine, *De cat. rud.* 20.34, and ACW 2.131 n. 218) and Confirmation.

[150] Cf. Lev. 10.1 f.

[151] 'Now': *scilicet*. Often the word scarcely calls for translation, being inserted merely for the rhythm (LCP 5.140; Grasmüller 44).

[152] 'God's teaching': *Dei traditione*. Before God's teaching became the Church's 'Tradition,' it was what God Himself, in the person of Christ, had 'handed down' to the Apostles, and for that reason could be called God's 'tradition' (the Pauline παράδοσις, e.g. 2 Thess. 3.6, quoted below, ch. 23; cf. 1 Cor. 11.23).

[153] Mark 7.9. 'reject the commandment': *reicitis mandatum*; Vulg. *irritum facitis praeceptum.*—'establish': *statuatis*; Vulg. *servetis.* Cyprian had already quoted this in *Ep.* 43.6. He also quotes it in *De dom. orat.* 2 and *Ep.* 63.14, 67.2, 74.3.

[154] 'crime ... no doubt, committed': *crimen quod admisisse ... videntur.* It is not a question of 'admitting guilt,' but of 'committing crime'; cf. Tertullian, *De pat.* 5: *aut quod crimen ante istud impatientiae admissum homini imputatur?*—On *videntur*, cf. LCP 6.50, which quotes Cyprian's *Ep.* 54.3 *nam etsi videntur in ecclesia esse zizania*: 'although

it is plain that . . .' (Watson 240 quotes this too, but here takes *videntur* as merely superfluous, as above, ch. 14 and n. 120).

[155] The translation given here is that of the second edition of the *De unitate* (cf. ch. 4 with notes, also Introd. 6–8). The first edition differs only slightly in this chapter, as follows: 'This crime is a greater one than that which was no doubt committed by *those who have sacrified* (*hi qui sacrificaverunt*), but these . . . to the full. *In the case of those others* (*illic*) the Church is being . . . appealed to, *but here* (*hic*) the Church is repudiated. *There* (*illic*), there may have been . . . pressure, but *here* (*hic*) the will persists in its guilt';—and so on, to the end of the chapter. This is more alive and actual: those with whom he was immediately concerned at the time were the schismatics, and so are '*hic*'; the lapsed who had sacrificed are referred to only by way of contrast, hence '*illic*.' When Cyprian revised the *De unitate*, he changed the *sacrificati* (who had happened to be the only lapsed then doing penance) to the more general term *lapsi*, and he inverted *hic* and *illic* throughout, as this was more correct grammatically; cf. Bévenot, '*Hi qui sacrificaverunt*,' JTS n.s. 5 (1954) 68–72.

[156] 'the will persists in its guilt': *voluntas tenetur in scelere*. The lapsed may, through torture or fear, have 'acted against his will'; the schismatic's action is fully deliberate.

[157] *Certe peccasse se hic et intellegit. Certe* is always initial, and is 'used not for restriction, but for assertion' (Watson 316)—a point missed by Grasmüller 37.

[158] 'upsets the holy ordinances of God': *Dei sacramenta disturbat.* It is unlikely that the sacraments are specifically referred to here. Poukens (in de Ghellinck 201) includes this passage under the heading 'Précepte,' yet qualifies it thus: '*commandements,* ou mieux *dispositions.*' It is the existing realities in the Church, not the commands of Christ as such, which are envisaged as having been upset—however much these realities are due to His commands. Cf. above, ch. 17: 'He is bearing arms against the Church, he is waging war upon God's *institutions*'; and ch. 18: 'any attempt made by the wicked deliberately to frustrate the *appointment* of God, is done against God Himself.'

[159] Cf. *Ep.* 19.2, which Cyprian quotes himself later, in *Ep.* 55.4.

[160] What Cyprian says in *Ep.* 55.28 f. and 57.4 might be taken as implying that even penitents, if not yet reconciled, were lost. But he does not say this, and his immediate concern there is with the importance of the Church's part in the forgiveness of sins.

[161] In *Ep.* 13.2–5 Cyprian had warned those who had had the courage to confess their faith, against the dangers of relaxation. Here he develops his thought in the light of subsequent experience.

[162] 'otherwise': *ceterum*, equivalent to *alioquin* (Grasmüller 38).

[163] Apoc. 3.11. 'lest another': *ne alius*; Vulg. *ut nemo*. The text is repeated in *Ad Fort.* 8 and *De bon. pat.* 13.

[164] 'never': *quod utique . . . non*. *Utique* equivalent to δή (Grasmüller 45).

[165] 'would be taken': *auferri posse*. A simple future could be replaced by some part of *posse* and the infinitive. Here the threat, *minaretur*, expects a future infinitive, but the clumsy *ablatum iri* is avoided by this circumlocution (LCP 9.102).

[166] 'it is not the ultimate achievement': *nec perficit laudem*; lit. 'it does not complete the [matter for] praise.'

[167] Matt. 10.22 and 24.13: *qui perseveraverit usque in finem hic salvus erit*. This is the same as the Vulg. and most O.L. MSS (but these have *ad* for *in*), whereas k, which normally gives the 'African' text, reads *qui sustinuerit usque ad finem, hic salvabitur*. This latter is probably what should be read at *Test.* 3.16 and *Ad Fort.* 8. In *Ep.* 12.1, 14.2, *Ad Fort.* 11, and *De bon. pat.* 13, the first verb is replaced by *toleraverit*. Under these circumstances, the difficulty of deciding what Cyprian's New Testament read here will escape no one (cf. von Soden 64, 76 f., 149. He prefers *salvabitur*, which is also found in *Ep.* 12 and 14 [85 f.], but recognizes that both forms might have existed side by side [158]).

[168] 'He is a confessor, no doubt': *confessor est*. Repeated four times in this chapter, to underline his danger and responsibilities.

[169] Cf. *De laps.* 20: 'those whom the Gospel enables to become martyrs, cannot act in opposition to the Gospel' (cf. *De laps.* 20 with n. 101 and especially *Ep.* 36.2, the letter from Rome there referred to).

[170] Luke 12.48. 'much is given': *multum datur* ; Vulg. *multum datum est*.—'is required': *quaeritur*; Vulg. *quaeretur*.—'on whom the more dignity is bestowed': *cui plus dignitatis adscribitur*; Vulg. *cui commendaverunt multum*.—'of him the more service is demanded': *plus de illo exigitur servitutis*; Vulg. *plus petent ab eo* (cf. von Soden 148).

One of the few instances where Cyprian quotes Scripture without explicitly stating so. He not infrequently incorporates Biblical phrases in his own sentences, but complete verses quoted without acknowledgment are rare (Watson 252 f.). However, the greater part of the 'quotation' is quite peculiar (cf. von Soden 177).

[171] Luke 14.11 and 18.14 (cf. Matt. 23.12). 'extolleth': *extollit* ; Vulg. *exaltat* or *exaltaverit*.—'humbleth himself': *humiliat se*; Vulg. *se humiliat* or *se humiliaverit*. In *Test.* 3.5 the better reading is *se humiliaverit*; *De dom. orat.* 6 reads *se humiliat*. Von Soden (86 f.) decides in favour of *se humiliaverit* with MS e and the Vulg. in Matt. 23.12.

[172] Cf. 1 Cor. 1.24.

[173] Cf. Phil. 2.8 f.

[174] 'yes, provided that': *sed si*; 'aber nur, wenn' (Grasmüller 64).

[175] 'to be blasphemed': cf. Rom. 2.24 (a quotation from Isa. 52.5); also 1 Tim. 6.1 and Titus 2.5. The effects of bad example were often described in this way.

[176] 'If nevertheless': *ceterum si*; cf. ch. 20 n. 162.

[177] 'in place of ... unfaithfulness': *fidem primam perfidia posteriore*; cf. *De laps.* 22 n. 109. Both meanings of *fides*, 'faith' and 'loyalty,' are involved here, as often elsewhere.

[178] *merita poenarum*: a *genetivus inversus*—cf. above, ch. 2 n. 13.

[179] Rom. 3.3 f. 'if some of them have fallen away from the faith': *si exciderunt a fide quidam illorum*; Vulg. *si quidam illorum non crediderunt.* —'unfaithfulness': *infidelitas*; Vulg. *incredulitas.*—'has ... made ... without effect': *evacuavit*; Vulg. *evacuabit.*—'For': *enim*; Vulg. *autem.* Cyprian quotes this text again in *Ep.* 59.7, 66.8, 67.8 (cf. *Sent. Episc.* 47).

[180] 'Our Lord's law and discipline': *legis ac disciplinae dominicae.* The last word is equivalent to *Domini*; cf. above ch. 17 n. 139.

[181] 'unity': *pace.* So too below: 'the unity of Christ.'

[182] *qui iuncti ... fuerunt.* The only instance, apparently, in Cyprian of the rare combination of the past participle with *fui* (cf. LCP 9.106–108, 118, and 6.29–38 for this and similar constructions).

[183] Cyprian's personification of the Church as the Mother of the faithful was no artificial abstraction—cf. above, ch. 6 n. 48, and *De laps.* ch. 2; also n. 10 there, for Prof. Plumpe's monograph *Mater Ecclesia.*

[184] 'the straight path of the way to heaven': *iter rectum viae caelestis.* An example, fairly common in late Latin, of the pleonastic *genetivus inhaerentiae*, where the genitive is of identical content with the substantive on which it depends; cf. LCP 5.81–85; 9.5.

[185] 2 Thess. 3.6. 'We bid you': *Praecipimus*; Vulg. *Denuntiamus.*— 'withdraw': *recedatis*; Vulg. *subtrahatis vos.*—'from all the brethren who walk': *ab omnibus fratribus ambulantibus*; Vulg. *ab omni fratre ambulante.* *Ep.* 59.20 has the same readings, as also *Test.* 3.68, though here the MS evidence varies, e.g. *discedatis* as well as *recedatis*, the word which Cyprian generally prefers (cf. von Soden 79).

[186] Eph. 5.6 f. 'deceive': *decipiat*; Vulg. *seducat.*—'because of that': *propterea*; Vulg. *propter haec.*—'upon the children of insolence': *super filios contumaciae*; Vulg. *in filios diffidentiae.*—'Be ye not therefore': *nolite ergo esse*; Vulg. *Nolite ergo effici.* Same text in *Ep.* 43.6 and 65.5.

[187] 'rather': *vel immo* (cf. Grasmüller 40).

[188] 'the wrong road of crime': *itinera erroris et criminis*; 'the true

way': *via veri itineris*. Two examples of the *genetivus definitivus*, a construction familiar in philosophical works, but otherwise not common save in Christian Latin: the genitive gives a more exact determination to the substantive on which it depends; cf. LCP 5.78–81; 9.5.

[188a] *concordiae glutino copulata*, cf. above, ch. 5 and n. 43.

[189] 'all hope of its salvation': *substantiam salutis*. From the Greek ὑπόστασις, the basis coming to stand for the essence, the 'substance' itself. Similarly in *De bon. pat.* 15: *sustinendi tolerandique substantiam* (cf. LCP 9.16).

[190] Ps. 33 (Heb. 34). 13–15. 'loveth': *amat*; Vulg. *diligit.*—'most blessed': *optimos*; Vulg. *bonos.*—'restrain': *contine*; Vulg. *prohibe.*—'deceitfully': *insidiose*; Vulg. *dolum.*—'Turn away': *Declina*; Vulg. *Diverte.*—'seek after': *quaere*; Vulg. *inquire.*—'pursue': *sequere*; Vulg. *persequere.* Verses 13 f. also occur in *Test.* 3.13, and v. 14 in *Ep.* 45.2. The latter and Hartel's apparatus in *Test.* 3.13 support the readings here. It has often been regretted that in *Testimonia* Hartel followed the Sessorianus MS A, which, interesting as it may be in itself, presents only a 'subsequent version'; the alterations 'are most evident in the Psalms, where half the quotations are entirely reworded' (Billen, *op. cit.* 3 f.; cf. Dom P. Capelle, *Le texte du psautier latin en Afrique* [Collectanea Biblica Latina 4 (Rome 1913)] 23–25; and on the present passage, 8, 30, 42, 78).

[191] John 14.27. 'I commit to you': *vobis dimitto*; Vulg. *relinquo vobis.* Quoted in *Test.* 3.3, where only W reads *dimitto*, the rest *remitto* (the vagaries of A can be neglected).

[192] Matt. 5.9. 'Blessed': *Beati*, as in Vulg. Throughout *Test.* μακάριος is represented not by *beatus* but by *felix*. If this is an exception, it will be because Cyprian, who no doubt often had occasion to quote this text in his sermons, always uses *beatus*, and not *felix*, in his own compositions (von Soden 69; cf. below, ch. 27 n. 202.—'they': *ipsi*. So also *Test.* 3.3, with k and f. Omitted in Vulg. and in the other O.L. MSS (Matzkow, *in loc.*).

[193] 'a common mind': *unanimitatis*.

[194] 'in the time of the Apostles': *sub apostolis*; cf. *De laps.* 6 n. 18.

[195] Acts 4.32. 'the crowd of those who had come to believe': *turba autem eorum qui crediderant*; Vulg. *multitudinis autem credentium.*—'acted with one mind and soul': *anima ac mente una agebant*; Vulg. *erat cor unum et anima una.* Cyprian gives the same reading in *Test.* 3.3, *De op. et el.* 25, and *Ep.* 11.3.

[196] Acts 1.14. 'all . . . with one mind': *omnes unanimes*; Vulg. *unanimiter.*—'who had been the mother of Jesus': *quae fuerat mater Iesu*; Vulg. *matre Jesu.*

197 'generosity of our charity': *largitas operationis*; cf. *De laps.* 35 and n. 171.

198 Cf. Matt. 6.20.

199 Luke 18.8. 'when He cometh': *cum venerit*; Vulg. *veniens*. Quoted also in *Ep.* 74.9, where, however, *putas* stands at the beginning of the sentence.

200 'sense of justice': *in lege iustitiae*. As in many other passages, '*lex* seems simply superfluous' (Watson 247).

201 'good works': *in opere*; cf. *De laps.* 35 n. 171.

202 Luke 12.35–37. 'girt': *adcincti*; Vulg. *praecincti.*—'burning': Vulg. adds *in manibus vestris.*—'when He shall come': *quando veniat*; Vulg *quando revertatur.*—'knocketh': Vulg. adds *confestim.*—'when He cometh' (second time): *adveniens*; Vulg. *cum venerit.* Also quoted in *Test.* 2.19, 3.11, and *Ad Fort.* 8. In all these, the preponderance of MSS favours *felices* for 'blessed,' as against *beati*, which is read here (as in Vulg.); cf. above, ch. 24 n. 192.

203 'it is impossible that we should be overcome': *opprimi . . . non possumus.* Cyprian, by using the indicative, creates the spirit of assurance with which he wants to end. It was all the easier to do so, because *posse* can replace both a subjunctive and a *future* (here most likely, because of the parallel *regnabimus*); in fact, *non possumus* might well be translated, simply, 'we shall not'; cf. LCP 6.48; cf. also n. 108 to *De laps.*

INDEX

INDEX

Aaron, 61

ablative, causal, with *in*, 94; instrumental, with *in*, 92, with *sub*, 101; of respect, with *in*, 88; of result, 100; *separativus*, with prep., 112 f.

Achias, 50

Adam, K., 76

Aemilius, 23, 83

agape, 115 f.

Alföldi, A., 74

almsdeeds, 21, 37, 66, 97 f.; reparation for sin, 41 f., 97 f.; *see* charity, *opera*, works

altar, heathen, *ara*; Christian, *altare*, 82, 87

Ambrose, St., 93

Ananias, Azarias, Misael, 38, 55, 95

apostasy, renunciation of faith, 3 f., 15, 18, 35, 39 f., 64, 81, 97

Apostles, 16, 18, 22, 41, 64, 66, 104; all with like power, 46, 102 f., 105, 123; all shepherds, 46, 105; forgive sins, 46; succession from, 103

Apuleius, 9 f.

Aristotle, *Hist. an.* 562 b: 112

Augustine, St., 76, 83, 109, 119
  C. Cresc. 3.36: 80; *C. Faust.* 16.31: 118; *De cat. rud.* 20.34: 119; *Serm.* 285: 83

aut and *vel*, 80, 94

authority, 9, 53, 107; of Bishop of Rome, 7; contempt for, 17, 101, 104; *see* bishop

Ayuso, T., 109

Azarias, the priest, 60

bad company, 39 f., 59, 65

Baer, J., 81

baptism, 9, 32, 78, 85, 95, 109; one, 47, 53, 107, 114; outside Church invalid, 114

baptismal controversy, 3, 7 f., 105 f., 108 f., 114

Bardy, G., 114

baths, 32, 37, 90 f., 94

Batiffol, P., 76

Baus, K., 78

Benson, E. W., 97

Beuron, 77

Bévenot, M., 75 f., 79, 85, 87, 89, 94, 97, 99, 103–105, 107, 113, 120

Billen, A. V., 88, 111, 123

bishop, authority of, 47, 50, 75, 86, 102, 104, 107; God's minister, 17, 28; intruded, 53, 106, 111; legitimately appointed, 103 f., 106; one in each place, 50, 111; controls penitential discipline, 73, 85 f.; and priest, 31, 33, 80, 90, 92; revolt against, 60, 104, 106 f.; shepherd, 50, 61; surgeon of souls, 24, 42

bishops, dependent on the source, 108, 115; discord among, 106; union of, 6, 8 f., 47, 75, 103, 106 f.; schismatic, 103

Blaise, A., 71, 82–85, 89, 113, 117

Blakeney, E. H., 11

Bludau, A., 109

Butler, B. C., 76, 108, 111

Byzantium, 81

Cain, 56

Cana, 110

Capelle, P., 123

Capitol, 19, 32, 81 f., 90

Capua, 81

Carthage, 81, 91, 107; synod at, 4

Casel, O., 74

Caspar, E., 76

Castus, 23, 83

catacombs, 95

cathedra Petri, 6, 46 f., 104 f., 108; necessary for Church membership, 47, 104

catholica, 74

Chapman, J., 75 f.

ANCIENT CHRISTIAN WRITERS

The Works of the Fathers in Translation

Edited by

J. QUASTEN, S.T.D., and J. C. PLUMPE, Ph.D.